PLANNING FOR EFFECTIVE FACULTY DEVELOPMENT

The Professional Practices in Adult Education and Human Resource Development Series explores issues and concerns of practitioners who work in the broad range of settings in adult and continuing education and human resource development.

The books are intended to provide information and strategies on how to make practice more effective for professionals and those they serve. They are written from a practical viewpoint and provide a forum for instructors, administrators, policy makers, counselors, trainers, managers, program and organizational developers, instructional designers, and other related professionals.

Editorial correspondence should be sent to

Editor
Professional Practices Series
Krieger Publishing Company
P.O. Box 9542
Melbourne, FL 32902-9542

PLANNING FOR EFFECTIVE FACULTY DEVELOPMENT

Using Adult Learning Strategies

Patricia A. Lawler
and
Kathleen P. King

KRIEGER PUBLISHING COMPANY
MALABAR, FLORIDA
2000

Original Edition 2000

Printed and Published by
KRIEGER PUBLISHING COMPANY
KRIEGER DRIVE
MALABAR, FLORIDA 32950

Library of Congress Cataloging-in-Publication Data

Lawler, Patricia A., 1944–
    Planning for effective faculty development : using adult learning
strategies / Patricia A. Lawler and Kathleen P. King.
        p.   cm.
    Includes bibliographical references and index.
    ISBN 1-57524-105-6 (hardcover)
    1. College teachers—Training of—United States. 2. Adult
education—United States. I. King, Kathleen P., 1958– II. Title.

LB1738 .L38 2000
374'.973—dc21

                                                            00-026717

10 9 8 7 6 5 4 3 2

CONTENTS

PREFACE

As colleges and universities are faced with the challenges of the new millennium, more and more attention is centered on the faculty of these institutions. Technology and distance education are changing classrooms and placing new and different demands on faculty. The student body, diverse in race, learning styles, ages, and cultures, demands new approaches to teaching and learning. Society calls for reform, demanding quality standards in not only teaching outcomes, but also in fiscal responsibility. At the heart of these challenges are the faculty. Once the unquestioned experts of their trade, they are now at the center of criticism and debate.

In addition to these challenges, we have seen in recent years more and more attention paid to professional development of faculty for the improvement of teaching and learning in higher education. Centers for teaching effectiveness and conferences on improving teaching have become popular, as evidenced by reading the higher education literature and promotions. And while there is not an abundance of literature or research, several authors address the topic of professional development (Boice, 1992; Brookfield, 1990, 1995; Cranton, 1996; Katz & Henry, 1996; Millis, 1994). However, as we assess this attention, there is something lacking. Rarely is the topic of faculty development informed by the theory and practice of adult learning.

The disciplines of adult education, adult learning, and adult development provide a broad theoretical basis to inform the education of adults in a variety of settings. Although this wealth of information has a strong theoretical and practical foundation, it has yet to be tapped for the professional development of faculty in colleges and universities and other adult education programs. As this information is reviewed, it becomes apparent that faculty strongly exemplify characteristics of adult learners. As professionals in the academy they are independent and self-directed in their work, and as they conduct their research they are interested in applying what they are learning to their work in the classroom.

Recent research on faculty development has shown that using the lens of adult education can be helpful in dealing with faculty development issues and concerns (Carroll, 1993; King, 1999; Lawler, DeCosmo, & Wilhite, 1996; Lawler & Wilhite, 1997; Licklider, Schnelker, & Fulton, 1997–1998; Wilhite, DeCosmo, & Lawler, 1996). Smylie (1995) notes that teacher education is "virtually uninformed by theories of adult learning and change" (p. 93). People who are responsible for instructional and professional development rarely view themselves as educators of adults (Cranton, 1996).

Planning for Effective Faculty Development will address these issues. The purpose of the book is to view faculty as adult learners and faculty development programs and initiatives as adult education. This is done by incorporating the literature and research from these disciplines to broaden and inform the perspectives of those responsible for faculty development in postsecondary institutions. It will combine the disciplines of adult education, adult learning, and program development to address what is missing in the literature. It introduces the concepts of adult learning and program development in adult education, and it sets forth a useful model with strategies for success. This book is designed as a practical guide for use by both administrators and teachers involved with faculty development. Since those responsible for faculty development usually have little background or training in adult education, adult learning, and program development, this book presents fundamental principles and illustrates their use in an understandable framework.

As faculty development programs are becoming more prolific in higher education today, people are being directed to create, teach, and run faculty development initiatives. Both new and experienced faculty developers face concerns about what needs to be done to be successful. Chapter 1 addresses these issues and concerns from our experience and the literature, provides an overview of what it takes to be successful, and demonstrates how using the model in this book will help faculty developers do what they need to do. This chapter addresses questions regarding defining faculty development, understanding faculty, and motivating faculty to participate in faculty development. Insights into the need for a new model for faculty development will conclude the chapter.

Chapter 2 presents the Adult Learning Model for Faculty Development, which has four stages grounded in adult learning and program planning principles. The theoretical and practical context for this model is presented as the principles are described. The model serves to create a conceptual framework from which to view the needs and issues that face faculty developers; this framework includes the principles and practices of adult learning and concepts and methodologies of program planning. The model is unique in that it views faculty development as adult learning, regards faculty as adult learners, and relies on program planning principles to construct and deliver an effective program. The remaining chapters move from theory to practice, as the practical concerns of faculty developers are discussed in the individual stages of the model and in the concluding guidelines for implementation.

Chapter 3 covers the five tasks related to the Preplanning Stage of the model: understanding organizational culture, identifying the role of the faculty developer, assessing needs, evaluating resources, and establishing goals. These tasks critical to program success are described, defined, and applied. Examples are drawn from faculty development experience, and issues and concerns of faculty developers are discussed.

In Chapter 4 the Planning Stage of the model is presented and the six tasks are identified: selecting a topic, identifying a presenter, preparing for delivery, preparing for support and transfer of learning, scheduling the event, and beginning the evaluation. The adult learning principles become increasingly prominent in this stage as the faculty development initiative continues to be developed.

Chapter 5 covers the four tasks related to the Delivery Stage of the model: building on the preparation, promoting the program, implementing adult learning principles, and monitoring the program. As this stage is described and defined, applications are made to typical situations. Recognizing the balance between the organization and faculty needs, effective communication channels are integral to the success of this stage. Within the framework of the model, adult learner needs, participatory and active learning programs, and the emphasis of application are discussed in the Delivery Stage.

The Follow-up Stage of the model includes three tasks: evaluating, continuing the learning, and assessing the faculty developer's role. At a time when many faculty development programs conclude with requisite evaluation forms, Chapter 6 proposes that much more may be done to extend the use and relevance of such programs. By creating meaningful evaluation, providing follow-up support and resources for the faculty, and considering their own roles in the process, faculty developers work to ensure successful programs.

In Chapter 7, faculty development is looked at from the perspective of how to ensure its effectiveness. The critical issues and challenges are discussed. In addition, guidelines for maintaining continuous effectiveness are presented. Finally, suggestions for the development and renewal of faculty developers are considered. This chapter provides the final step in making the Adult Learning Model for Faculty Development operational for the reader.

The primary audience for this volume includes faculty development practitioners and other professional adult educators who are responsible for developing and presenting faculty professional development initiatives in postsecondary institutions, noncollegiate institutions and organizations such as literacy councils, health and community education programs, and state and city boards of adult education. Examples of such individuals are faculty developers, instructional specialists, faculty, administrators, consultants, those working in centers for teaching effectiveness and professional development, and higher education leaders interested in initiating such programs. Deans and directors of both academic units and continuing education programs responsible for hiring, training, and evaluating full-time and adjunct faculty will also benefit from this volume. It can also serve as a text for graduate education courses in faculty, staff, or professional development.

We recognize that faculty development is done in many different contexts and formats. What this book proposes is the use of a model for faculty development that is informed by and consistent with adult learning principles. Building on the strength of the literature, the integration of adult learning principles creates a robust model that may be adapted to innumerable settings. We hope to let you see faculty development through our eyes as we discuss problem scenarios and possible solutions in each chapter. The faculty bring a rich tradition and experience to faculty development initiatives. It is our hope that faculty developers will be better able to serve the faculty, the organizations, and the learners by considering this alternative model.

ACKNOWLEDGMENTS

Many individuals and institutions helped us in this project. We are grateful to all, but wish to recognize those who made special contributions. John Fielder and Joe Palombo patiently edited our many drafts of the book, graduate students at Widener University and Fordham University provided research assistance, Barbara Mangos designed the graphics, and Michael Galbraith and Mary Roberts at Krieger Publishing encouraged us and provided many useful suggestions.

From Patricia Lawler:
Widener University strongly supports faculty development and encouraged me to work with Arlene DeCosmo, Dean of University College, and Stephen Wilhite, Dean of the School of Human Service Professions. Our research on faculty as adult learners was an exciting collaboration and inspiration for this book. Special thanks to John Fielder, whose patience, support, advice and love helped me over the many rough spots.

From Kathleen King:
Thank you to the many faculty members and teachers who have been in my classes and workshops. They have inspired me to pursue a research agenda on professional development in teacher education and faculty development. Thank you to the faculty members at Fordham University who have been an encouragement in pursuing this book. In addition, I want to express special thanks to Sharon Sanquist for her support when the path to completion seemed long. Finally, my heartfelt thanks are extended to the colleagues and friends who provided feedback and room for dialogue throughout the creative process.

THE AUTHORS

Patricia A. Lawler is an Associate Professor in the Center for Education at Widener University in Chester, Pennsylvania. She received her Ed.D. from Teachers College, Columbia University, New York, in adult and continuing higher education. She received her B.A. in psychology from the College of New Rochelle, New York and her M.S. in counseling from Villanova University.

Lawler's teaching responsibilities are in the graduate programs at Widener University in the areas of adult education and leadership in higher education. They focus on adult learning, program planning, higher education administration, women's education, and alternative models of education. She is the author of *The Keys to Adult Learning: Theory and Practical Strategies* and numerous articles and papers. Lawler has made numerous presentations, both invited and refereed, at regional, national, and international conferences.

Her research has centered on ethical issues in adult and continuing higher education. She, along with John Fielder, Ph.D., Professor of Philosophy, Villanova University, has conducted research with the Association for Continuing Higher Education. Several of their articles on ethical issues have been published in *The Journal of Continuing Higher Education*. Their work was a major contribution in the association's development and adoption of their Code of Ethics.

Lawler has been designing and delivering faculty and staff development for over ten years. Her expertise is grounded in her doctoral work at Teachers College, Columbia University, where she collaboratively developed a set of principles of adult education. Her work includes faculty development workshops with law professors, and adjunct and full-time faculty on such topics as cooperative learning, gender issues, learning styles and personality types. Taking her expertise into the corporate and non-profit world, she has been responsible for developing and delivering programs for an accounting firm and a national mentoring organization. She has also been involved with the faculty development initiative at Widener University. There she has presented workshops and conducted research.

Lawler has held numerous leadership positions, both regionally and nationally with the Association for Continuing Higher Education and assumed the presidency in 1999. In 1994 she was awarded the Association for Continuing Higher Education Region IV Adult Educator of the Year Award. She serves on the editorial board of *PAACE Journal of Lifelong Learning* and *New Horizons in Adult Education*. Lawler also reviews proposals for several national and regional conferences.

Prior to her joining the faculty at Widener University, Lawler was an administrator at Chestnut Hill College and Villanova University. She also has extensive experience in consulting and training in both the corporate and nonprofit arenas.

Kathleen P. King is an Assistant Professor and Program Coordinator of Adult Education and Human Resource Development and Program Director of Instructional Technology Professional Development at Fordham University's Graduate School of Education, New York, New York. She received her Ed.D. in higher education and M.Ed. in adult education from Widener University, Chester, Pennsylvania. Her B.A. is in biochemistry from Brown University, Providence, Rhode Island, and her M.A. in missions from Columbia International University, South Carolina. Her primary teaching areas have been program planning, adult and distance education, educational technology, administration of adult education programs, and adult learning. Her research interests lie in the areas of transformational learning, educational technology, faculty development, and teacher education.

Since 1990, she has planned, designed, and conducted faculty and staff development for several institutions and companies. In the past, she has taught at Widener University, Holy Family College, and the Pennsylvania Institute of Technology.

All totaled, King has over 20 years experience in adult education and teacher training in different settings.

King has combined her knowledge of adult education with computer technology expertise. In her work in faculty and staff development, she has consistently incorporated principles of adult education in classes on educational technology, presentation development, Internet applications, and technology instruction. These classes have been conducted in higher education, adult education, and secondary education institutions as well as in business settings.

King is the author of *A Guide to Perspective Transformation and Learning Activities: The Learning Activities Survey* and numerous articles, chapters, and published conference proceedings. She has made invited and refereed presentations at regional and national conferences on her areas of research and study. King is on the editorial boards of *New Horizons in Adult Education* and *Adult Basic Education,* participates in reviewing articles and papers for several journals and conferences, and is the coeditor of the proceedings of adult education research conferences.

CHAPTER 1

Becoming a Successful Faculty Developer

Joan Brentwood, the new president of Eastwood Community College, was well aware of the many challenges facing her small, rural, community college. Advancing technology, changing student demographics, shifts in funding, and an aging faculty were right at the top of her list. The college's Strategic Planning Committee recommended a campuswide faculty development initiative to meet these challenges, improve teaching effectiveness, and implement an important aspect of the mission of the college, building a learning community. After conferring with several of her fellow presidents at an international conference, Dr. Brentwood was well aware of the existence of faculty development programs, teaching and learning centers in the United States, and staff development initiatives in Great Britain. Her first task was to identify the appropriate person on campus to plan and implement a program for faculty and to work with the college's development office to raise funds to support such an effort. Her second task was to reflect on what this person would need to know to become a successful faculty developer at Eastwood. It was time to make decisions and provide guidance.

This scenario, like the many others we relate throughout the book, illustrates a current situation in which critical decisions can lead to success or failure. As faculty development programs are becoming more and more common in higher education today, people are being chosen to create and administer faculty development centers and initiatives and teach in faculty development programs. Where do they learn how to do this? What knowledge and skills do they need to be successful? What exactly is the role of a faculty developer? Legends and university folklore abound with horror stories about inadequate workshops, poor planning, and of course, unmotivated faculty. But what is the reality? And how can we plan successful programs and motivate faculty not only to attend and learn, but also to change?

This chapter will set the stage for becoming a successful faculty developer by providing an introduction to this critical function within our colleges and universities. We will then explore the professional culture of faculty to afford an understanding of the work and development issues of this segment of the university community. These issues and concerns are at the heart of many of the faculty development initiatives today and crucial in our understanding of what faculty need to do to get their job done. Another question is, how do we motivate faculty to come to workshops on campus and most of all to implement what they have learned? The chapter would be incomplete without addressing this important topic.

Our educational backgrounds in adult learning and our experiences in adult education and faculty development have led us to believe that a new paradigm is necessary for faculty development. So, we conclude the chapter with a challenge to the reader by asking you to begin thinking of the faculty as adult learners, faculty development as adult education, and yourself as an adult educator. This will entail bringing the concepts and resources from the discipline of adult education to this process. The Adult Learning Model for Faculty Development presented in Chapter 2 and described throughout the following chapters will assist you in this new thinking and provide a systematic framework for becoming a successful faculty developer.

WHAT IS FACULTY DEVELOPMENT?

Historically, faculty development in its broadest sense has been around since the 19th century when Harvard began sabbatical leaves to support faculty in gaining competence in their disciplines (Eble & McKeachie, 1985). However, Gaff and Simpson (1994) tell us that it was only at the beginning of the 20th century that criteria for selecting and retraining college professors moved away from "religious faith or affiliation, character, and other personal qualities" (p. 167) to professional standards which include advanced degrees and knowledge of an academic discipline. Because faculty were and are considered experts in their academic disciplines, this focus took precedence over instructional skills and aptitude. Colleges and universities found ways to support faculty as they developed expertise in their disciplines and gained new knowledge in their fields of study. Little attention was paid to "the improvement of instruction" (Gaff, 1976, p. 12). Activities to support professional development centered on "keeping up to date in their fields" (Gaff & Simpson, 1994, p. 168). Examples of such activities include sabbaticals and leaves, travel and research funding, grants, fellowships, and attendance at professional meetings. Gaff (1976) defined faculty development "as enhancing the talents, expanding the interests, and improving the competence and otherwise facilitating the professional and personal growth of faculty members, particularly in their roles as instructors" (p. 14). Baiocco and DeWaters (1995) report that while these activities and sporadic workshop presentations in the past may have been thought of as adequate to meet the needs of the faculty as they grew professionally in their disciplines, in today's higher education climate there is greater attention on professional growth in teaching effectiveness. This calls for a new kind of faculty development. For the past few decades, efforts in faculty development have been leading up to this point.

Faculty development began moving in this new direction in the 1970s. Hubbard and Atkins (1995) summarize the changes.

> Early faculty development efforts of the 1970's attempted to improve institutional effectiveness primarily by addressing the disciplinary expertise or pedagogical skills of faculty members. Subsequent approaches focused on understanding the complexity of the teaching/learning process and expanding faculty awareness of new emerging information about cognition and development. In recent years, there has been a re-

newed interest in both personal and organizational approaches that address issues of faculty vitality and renewal. (p. 118)

It was during the 1980s that we began to see the establishment of instructional development centers and centers for teaching and learning, which focused on developing faculty and their expertise in classroom practices (Gaff & Simpson, 1994; Millis, 1994; Simpson, 1990). This interest in faculty development continued through the 1990s and became much more critical as the challenges facing higher education at the end of the 20th century increased and diversified. The focus of much of the literature in faculty development has been on student learning, and while writers suggest that understanding student learning should be the top priority in faculty development, faculty themselves may not agree, leading to a conflict of needs (Knapper, 1995).

Millis (1994) cites challenges to the academy and widespread social changes as compelling reasons to expand faculty development in the future. Her list of five reasons has been supported in the literature (Baiocco & DeWaters, 1998; Lawler & Wilhite, 1997; Rowley, Lujan, & Dolence, 1997):

1. Changing expectations about the quality of undergraduate education

2. Changing social needs

3. Changing technology and its impact on teaching and learning

4. Changing student populations

5. Changing paradigms in teaching and learning (Millis, 1994, pp. 454–457)

Each of these challenges requires faculty and the university to rethink many of the traditional teaching strategies. Whether a professor is converting a syllabus from paper to electronic technology or substituting a multimedia presentation for the blackboard and chalk, technology is affecting how faculty get the job done. In an era where the traditional-aged student may be the expert when it comes to computers and other technologies, how do faculty who grew up with typewriters and the U.S. Postal Service become proficient in this new complex technological world? This change, along with the changes in student populations, is creating a new learning challenge for the faculty. Faculty on our campuses today remain predominately white, male, and middle class (Blackburn & Lawrence, 1995), whereas the student population has become increasingly diverse. College students are now older, attending part-time, and from various social classes. Many are first generation college and many others come from a wide spectrum of racial and ethnic groups, including new immigrants (Merriam & Brockett, 1997). These students may not share their professors' values or their work ethic, may be unfamiliar with the academic culture and its rules, and may be more consumer oriented (Baiocco & DeWaters, 1998).

While faculty development initiatives have been on the increase to address these challenges, there has been little research to aid in the understanding of how faculty development works. Maxwell and Kazlauskas (1992) presented a review of research and found that most information centered on the organizational environment and the faculty development programs themselves. This information included program descriptions, but little about the changes in teachers or students. Maxwell and Kazlauskas observed that workshops were the primary delivery mode and concluded, "although these programs are prevalent at colleges throughout the nation, faculty participation is low" (p. 356). They made one other important conclusion, which has meaning for us as we think about effective faculty development. "Faculty development programs often emphasize general teaching skills, whereas faculty members tend to be concerned with disciplinary knowledge and specific teaching tasks" (p. 356). Wilhite, DeCosmo, and Lawler (1996) came to a similar conclusion after surveying faculty who had attended faculty development workshops on active learning and technology. These faculty members were concerned with immediate application in their own discipline with specific examples, not generalized methodology.

In an attempt to gain more information about the incidence and effectiveness of faculty development, Baiocco and De-

Waters (1995) surveyed a sample of American Association of University Professors (AAUP) presidents in 435 colleges and universities nationwide. They reported that while it is estimated that only "one-third of all higher education institutions have some form of organized faculty development, 71 percent of the AAUP sample reported that they had a comprehensive program" (p. 38). However, their definition of a comprehensive program included "institutional funding for at least three of the following activities: travel, research, consultant-led workshops, faculty-led workshops, development personnel/mentor, and equipment/office/space/supplies" (p. 38). Later Baiocco and DeWaters (1998) presented a comprehensive analysis of faculty development. They came to the conclusion that "higher education institutions must increase efforts and offer a radically different faculty development program to ensure that faculty will understand the changing nature of the student population, education and their respective disciplines" (p. 40). This call for change demands that we move away from a deficit model of development toward one of professional development and growth.

Like many organizations in our society, colleges and universities are interested in the performance and output of their workers. Training and staff development have been seen as one way to improve these attributes. However, much of this training has been conceived as remediation. Faculty development has been used by administrators to address the "perceived inadequacy of the faculty" (Hawthorne & Smith, 1994, p. 181). Candy (1996) reports that seeing faculty development initiatives as "fundamentally deficit-oriented, designed to remedy shortcomings in people's current level of skill . . . [is] flawed and impoverished" (p. 8). He urges us to take a more comprehensive view which would include a proactive approach and a reflective awareness of practice. We are learning today that a deficit model of training and development may not be as effective as one which comes from a proactive and positive growth approach. Hawthorne and Smith (1994) report that faculty development promotes institutional excellence. Faculty development that is participated in for its own sake creates an environment that sustains and nurtures the faculty.

In the past, professional development for faculty has been seen as an answer to challenges facing the academy. We have all heard the cry, "if we could only get the faculty to change this . . . then everything would be better." But research has shown that while faculty development initiatives are warranted and in some cases well-regarded (Baiocco & DeWaters, 1998; Chism & Szabo, 1997–1998), they have not been connected with personal (faculty) or institutional change. Many of the critiques of past and current faculty development offerings focus on the sporadic, unsystematic manner of organization. Another focus of critiques is the unrelatedness of either content or process with the needs of the faculty or what they consider important for improving their professional practice. This book addresses these issues by offering a systematic plan for effective faculty development and most important, it starts with the faculty. Let us turn now to look at the faculty and their professional life.

WHO ARE THE FACULTY?

One of the basic premises of adult learning theory and practice (Galbraith, 1998; Lawler, 1991; Merriam & Caffarella, 1999) is to start with the adult learners who are the potential participants and to identify their characteristics. Getting to know the participants and their learning needs, as well as their organizational and professional culture and context, facilitates effective practice in creating and delivering faculty development programs. Although we will be looking at this process in detail in later chapters, it is important to provide an overview of faculty as workers and as learners. Without that context we may be making assumptions that can derail even our best efforts in program planning. In this section we will look at the faculty, their work culture, how they get their work done, and how they perceive their professional roles and responsibilities.

Originally, professors were masters of subject knowledge who professed this knowledge to young people. Their work was a life commitment to acquiring and incorporating new knowledge and they did this work in the university whose mandate it was to create and disseminate knowledge. Like the ministry, the professorate was considered a vocation, a calling. Professors were lifelong learners who, as part of their professional responsibilities, were required to read and research new knowledge to incorporate into their daily work. However, this training as researchers offered little grounding in educational or pedagogical theory (Knapper, 1995). Although this tradition is very much a part of today's colleges and universities, faculty no longer can pursue only their academic discipline. Accountability, changes in demographics, and new technology are demanding new ways of teaching and accumulating knowledge.

For us, as we consider being effective faculty developers, it is imperative that we start with a basic understanding of what type of person is attracted to this career and the work that it entails. Schneider and Zalesny (1982) offer a perspective on who finds academic life a rewarding career choice. They "propose that those attracted to and potentially gratified by the relatively unstructured world of academe would be mature individuals with strong self-actualization, growth, and achievement needs, for whom work is as natural as play, and who enjoy a challenge and taking a moderate risk" (p. 38). This unstructured world includes a work schedule that few outside the academy may understand. The academic year with its semesters and breaks provides different time patterns for faculty to get their work done. Research, writing, and preparing for class may occur over breaks and in the summer, while service, teaching, and working directly with students occur during the semester. Working within their academic disciplines offers opportunities for pursuing ideas and knowledge acquisition. Blackburn and Lawrence (1995) found in their study that faculty work long hours and are concerned with the lack of time they have to fullfill their professional responsibilities.

Historically, our universities and colleges have been providers of knowledge and skills from a wide variety of disciplines. The faculty are the experts and purveyors of this information, which is then passed on to students in classes and to the academic community in writing (Rowley, Lujan, & Dolence, 1997). Within this role, "academics are encouraged to be autonomous in their pursuit and dissemination of knowledge" (Simpson, 1990, p. 24). In fact, faculty are rewarded for individual accomplishments; and in recent research studies, new faculty were found to feel isolated. This isolation is characteristic of the daily work life of faculty where their responsibilities include preparing for classes and teaching. While research and service are also required of faculty, much time goes into preparing classes and teaching courses (Luce & Murray, 1997–1998; Paulsen & Feldman, 1995; Sorcinelli, 1994). With little or no guidance on how to teach or prepare for classes, faculty replicate the process that they have experienced as learners. This fact has changed little over the years (Knapper, 1995; Seldin, 1990).

While each individual institution has a unique faculty with its own demographic characteristics, it is helpful to understand the larger picture of the professorate. Blackburn and Lawrence's (1995) research on faculty at work reports that faculty members are getting older and that across the disciplines there are fewer women and minorities especially at the higher ranks, than white males. "Today, tenured faculty members, 50 years of age or older, constitute approximately half of the full-time faculty at colleges and universities across the United States" (Crawley, 1995, p. 65). Information on adult development and adult learning can help us understand the learning needs of this unique population. Throughout this book we will incorporate this information in practical ways to assist the faculty developer.

HOW DO WE MOTIVATE FACULTY?

In our seminars and workshops on faculty development, the most asked question is, how do we motivate faculty? Participants and colleagues see this as their biggest challenge. Whether we are interested in getting consumers to buy a new product, our children to clean up their bedrooms, or the faculty to attend a workshop, motivation is a topic that spans both the academic world and the practical daily lives of all of us. The fields of education, psychology, human development, and business have all contributed to the literature. There are references to help us understand motivation in general and more specifically how to motivate faculty to participate in professional development activities that go beyond the traditional sabbaticals and meetings toward the goal of improving teaching and learning in the classroom.

Wlodkowski (1993) refers to motivation as an elusive concept that theorists and educators have been eager to define and understand. He reports that the term has been used "to describe those processes that can (a) arouse and instigate behavior, (b) give direction or purpose to behavior, (c) continue to allow behavior to persist, and (d) lead to choosing or preferring a particular behavior" (p. 2). As faculty developers, we are interested in motivating faculty to come to programs and find something worthwhile that will lead to new behaviors, such as new teaching methods in the classroom. So we want the faculty to choose the program offering and also to see value in the content enough to adopt and persist in a new behavior.

Malcolm Knowles, a renowned writer in adult education, links motivation with learners' needs (Knowles, 1980). He sees the role of adult educators as assisting learners, in this case the faculty, in achieving their goals. Knowles emphasizes the connection we should make between learners' needs and successful outcomes. If the learners do not make this connection between their need to learn and the content and process of the program, there may be little motivation to continue. Knowles also emphasizes the importance of choice and adults' need for control over their learning choices. As we will see in future chapters, the concept of need and the faculty's input into what programming should entail, when it should occur, and how it should be delivered are crucial for effective programming.

Motivating faculty therefore starts with identifying their learning needs. How we work within organizations and certainly the organizations' needs also require consideration. Yet, if our faculty do not perceive that their voices are heard and that they have a choice, all of our efforts at encouraging participation and transfer of learning may fail.

Wlodkowski (1993) recommends that we take into account a learner's attitude and competence when developing strategies for motivation. This is particularly important in working with faculty. We must remember that faculty are in the education business, are "experts" in their disciplines, and may have been teaching for quite some time, as the above demographics exhibited. Their autonomy includes assessing their own needs. "Faculty frequently find the process of designing instruction, conducting research, and teaching to be development themselves in the sense that these activities keep them current in content and methods, stimulate their enthusiasm, and keep them attended to changing institutional needs" (Hawthorne & Smith, 1994, p. 185). Therefore, their motivation for pursuing faculty development activities may not be in alignment with those of administration. If there is a prevailing attitude that this new learning will not enhance their professional life or that there is little support, affirmation, or reward, the faculty may see little or no need to attend or learn.

> Those who value tenure, promotion, and other rewards that the university offers will tend to maximize behaviors that help to attain those rewards and minimize behaviors that do not. A faculty development program that addresses behaviors that are irrelevant to the rewards system has little chance of success, except among those who are unconcerned about the reward structure. (Watson & Grossman, 1994, p. 469)

It is crucial that we as faculty developers understand the reward system within our own institution. If a faculty member does not see connections between the faculty development program, changing behavior as a result of new learning, and then appropriate affirmation and reward to adopting new behaviors, there may be little motivation to attend. Angelo (1994) reports that "many faculty won't invest time and energy in programs not directly related to their immediate, very specific teaching needs" (p. 5). He urges us to look beyond extrinsic rewards, such as money and recognition. He cites the importance of intrinsic rewards such as "professional pride, intellectual challenge, the fulfillment that comes from helping students" (p. 5). Focusing on the faculty and their motivations, including their values and needs will help us overcome barriers to change. "When the motivation to improve is intrinsic, the results are very different.

The effects on instruction are more enduring, faculty attitudes are more positive and faculty commitments to continued improvement are stronger" (Weimer, 1990, p. 23).

Ekroth (1990) cites several reasons why faculty do not change. She reports that our institutions have both a physical culture and a social culture, which have not changed over time, and which continue to be the guardians of tradition. Also within the academy, the reward systems for faculty may not be consistent with the faculty development offerings. Faculty also may see little incentive for change. And as with all of us, change requires risk taking, discomfort, and anxiety. "Behavior that is familiar feels comfortable, and what feels comfortable resists change" (Ekroth, 1990). Addressing these concerns by promoting risk taking and enhancing institutional support, especially with senior faculty, can add to the effectiveness of the professional development initiative (Crawley, 1995).

Understanding motivation and the characteristics of our potential participants provides us with a starting point from which we can develop effective programming. We believe that conceiving of faculty development as adult education and seeing the faculty as adult learners are crucial for motivation and the outcomes of a motivated learner. Throughout this book we will offer strategies and suggestions for being both effective and successful.

BECOMING SUCCESSFUL

As we approach the prospect of actually planning and delivering professional development activities on campus, we are of course concerned with being successful in our role as faculty developers. Our goal should be to contribute welcomed initiatives and effective programs. We aim to create a positive experience for the faculty that will encourage the use of new ideas. We are interested in engaging the faculty not only in single learning events, but also in creating a culture that will promote enthusiasm for continued learning and professional growth. This is how we define successful faculty development. We believe we can reach this goal by integrating the theories of adult learning and adult education program planning principles into faculty development. This requires a new perspective in which we understand the purpose and goals of our work as faculty developers, along with a collaborative environment within the institution. Baiocco and DeWaters (1998) maintain that faculty development has not been particularly effective due to lack of cohesion, inconsistent offerings, and the following of educational fads. Their research has shown "a spotty record of success of traditional faculty development programs" (Baiocco & DeWaters, 1998, p. 34). They call for a radically different perspective on faculty development. We agree with their call for this new perspective and have developed a cohesive and comprehensive model that will facilitate success.

Becoming successful as a faculty developer requires attention to several aspects of faculty development and program planning that may not have been considered in the past. As we strive to complete our tasks to deliver a program or initiative on schedule, we may not have given much thought to the larger picture of what faculty development means for our institution. As we look at the important issues and concerns that surround our universities and colleges today, faculty developers need to take a holistic approach and see their role as an integral part of the life of the institution. Watson and Grossman (1994) encourage faculty developers to provide a vision for effective faculty development that includes crucial aspects such as cooperation across the campus, administrative support, and utilization of the expertise of the faculty themselves. Other authors have provided their perspectives on successful faculty development. Yet there has been relatively little research to provide us with benchmarks and direction. In fact Angelo (1994) reports that we are more likely to find a lack of leadership, support, commitment, and planning for success in faculty development initiatives. From his extensive work with faculty development he reports that faculty "are more apt to respect well-planned, well-organized, and well-led enterprises" (p. 5). This book provides a vehicle to create such enterprises. This model, the Adult Learning Model for Faculty Development, will contribute to success as it presents a change in perspective regarding faculty development that is grounded in adult learning theory and faculty development practice.

Another aspect that contributes to success is being acutely aware of the faculty and their needs. Brookfield (1995) reports that "much of faculty development is done *to* teachers by people defined as outside experts. The focus of these efforts is the acquisition by teachers of skills, insights, or knowledge that someone else has defined as being good for them" (p. 66). He encourages us to shift this perspective and include the faculty's own experiences as teachers in both the planning and delivery of faculty development programs. Wedman and Strathe (1985) also agree that the faculty are the "key factor to be accounted for in a faculty development effort" (p. 16). It is imperative that we recognize the faculty as individuals in this process of learning, utilizing their experiences not only as teachers and members of the academy, but also as learners. Even when innovations and new techniques are driving the faculty development effort, we must not lose sight of the faculty's perception of what is needed to be effective in their work. Morgan, Phelps, and Pritchard (1995) see the importance for faculty developers to not only understand the needs of the faculty, but also appreciate who they are. This is integral to strong leadership and vision. Strong leadership is based on being credible, which means understanding the needs of the faculty.

Along with these aspects there has been a call to use the constructs of adult education and adult learning in the work of faculty development (Carroll, 1993; Gordon & Levinson, 1990; Lawler & Wilhite, 1997; Licklider, Schneiker, & Fulton, 1997–1998). It is imperative that we recognize that the faculty strongly exemplify the characteristics of adult learners as described in the literature (Cross, 1981; Knowles, 1980, 1992; Lawler, 1991). Faculty, by nature of their profession, are self-directed in their work, independent and autonomous in getting their job done, and collaboratively participate in the policy and governance of the university. Their training as scholars and researchers promotes these characteristics. Failed faculty development initiatives appear to treat the faculty, not as adult learners, but as either traditional dependent learners or as employees in a corporate setting.

The literature from adult education and adult learning provides us with over 50 years of research and practice of working with adult learners in a variety of settings. It is now time to utilize these important and useful resources in the process of faculty development. If, as we have seen, there have been ineffective, inconsistent, and spotty efforts, then it is time to establish a new paradigm for success. We offer the Adult Learning Model for Faculty Development to do just that. This model is also distinctive in taking into consideration the culture of education. It builds on the implications of motivating people to learn and implement their learning and see it as a positive experience. It also addresses the imperatives which Brookfield (1995), Morgan, Phelps and Pritchard (1995), and Baiocco and De-Waters (1998) call for in working with faculty.

The Adult Learning Model for Faculty Development offers a formed and consistent framework for doing faculty development, which takes into consideration the institution, the faculty, and organizational needs. It offers specific tasks to guide the faculty developer through the process; these tasks will be discussed in full as we consider the separate stages of the model. So many times we get caught up in the rush to produce programs that we may neglect small but important steps that may lead to disaster. A step-by-step approach to avoid such problems is enhanced by the Faculty Development Checklist and the Faculty Developer's Self-Assessment Tool. These tools will be discussed in Chapter 7 and can be found in Appendix A and Appendix B.

President Brentwood has a challenge before her. Both she and her faculty developer are interested in creating a successful faculty development initiative for Eastwood Community College. The Adult Learning Model for Faculty Development provides an informed and helpful model that includes these concerns as it guides the faculty developer in creating successful and effective programs. The use of this model necessitates a change in perspective for President Brentwood and her college. To meet her challenges and the ones you may have in your institution, we urge you to look at the faculty as adult learners, the programming for faculty as an adult education enterprise, and yourself as an adult educator. In Chapter 2, we provide a foundation in adult learning so that you may better comprehend your new role and perspective. With this understanding you will be well equipped to begin the process of program planning for faculty. The Adult Learning Model for Faculty Development facilitates this process and offers theoretical foundations, specific tasks, short case studies, and guidelines to illustrate how the model works in practice.

CHAPTER 2

Programming for Faculty Development

As more and more colleges and universities take on the challenge of professional development for their faculty, it is imperative that those responsible be prepared to develop and deliver effective programs. Whether the developer is working out of a teaching and learning center where programs are ongoing, or has just been appointed a new administrative task of presenting the first on-campus faculty development event, challenges abound. There is a movement to provide the professorate with new opportunities to learn about technology, active learning, changing classroom demographics, and innovative instructional methodology. As more colleges and universities offer seminars, workshops, and conferences for faculty and as faculty desire opportunities to improve their professional practice, there is a need for guidance to produce effective and successful programs.

Those responsible for the creation, design, and delivery of programs are faced with specific challenges. Concerns about faculty motivation, appropriate topics, delivery systems, and utilization of the learning in the classroom are but a few. One way to meet the challenges of faculty development is to approach it in a systematic manner using an adult education program planning perspective. We then see the faculty as adult learners and faculty development as an adult education activity. The research, theory, and practice from the discipline of adult education provide a rich resource to create a systematic plan which offers faculty developers a new and different position from which to plan faculty development programs. This plan is captured in the Adult Learning Model for Faculty Development.

This chapter will first present research, theory, and practice from the field of adult education, specifically principles of adult learning and concepts of program planning. For those unfamiliar with the discipline, it provides a background and grounding in the theoretical concepts, which make this programming planning model unique. For those versed in the field, it offers a review of critical theories and a new schema for practical use. Following this foundation in adult education, The Adult Learning Model for Faculty Development will be presented. Its foundation in adult learning will be explored and illustrated and adult education programming principles will be described. The four stages of this integrative model will be introduced. Each stage will then be described in detail with practical implications in Chapters 3 through 6. The model is unique in that it approaches faculty development as adult learning, it looks at faculty as adult learners, and it relies on program planning principles to construct and deliver effective programs.

ADULT EDUCATION'S CONTRIBUTION TO FACULTY DEVELOPMENT

As early as the 1920s Eduard Lindeman (1961) urged us to consider the important aspects of adult education and its meaning for us as we progress through adulthood and our professional lives. Throughout this century scholars, practitioners, and researchers have continually increased their focus on how adults learn and develop over their lifespan. In the 1960s, Malcolm Knowles (1980, 1989) began to incorporate this information into the practice of adult education and used the term *andragogy* to best describe the "art and science of teaching adults." Since then, a substantial body of knowledge has emerged informing the practice of adult education in a variety of settings. It is this body of knowledge that we have accessed and applied to the practice of faculty development to create the Adult Learning Model for Faculty Development. First we will explore the adult learning principles that have been incorporated into the model. We will then go on to present the concepts of adult education program planning that provide a crucial foundation for the model.

Adult Learning

If we are to consider faculty as adult learners, then an understanding of adult learners, their characteristics and experience, is crucial for our model. As adults age, they become more and more diverse in their experiences (Lawler, 1991; Merriam & Caffarella, 1999). In other words, the older we are, the more we are different from each other. Our past personal and professional experiences continually impact our present experiences. This concept has many implications for faculty development as the adult learners, the faculty, bring their background and experience to any program we may plan (Knowles, 1980, 1989). How do we take advantage of this experience and not see this diversity among our faculty as a barrier to successful programming? First, we can understand that adults will participate in educational programming for a variety of reasons, many of which may be an interaction between themselves and their sociocultural world (Jarvis, 1995). Faculty, trained in their disciplines and acculturated into the academic community, have unique characteristics which will influence their educational development and learning. Traditionally, faculty seek continued learning to enhance their specific discipline, gain new knowledge in their field and uncover new ideas and information through research. Today's faculty development initiatives, which center on teaching methods, technology, and new paradigms for the classroom, are very different from previous experiences faculty may have had. Those experiences have traditionally been concerned with academic disciplines and faculty research. We need to understand then that faculty may have little or no experience with new ideas about the process of teaching, especially instructional methodology little used within their own academic discipline (Brookfield, 1990).

In developing programs for adults, it is imperative to consider the social context and multiple interests working within complex organizations (Cervero & Wilson, 1994). These may have critical implications for not only the content of an educational program, but also how it should be taught. Again, academic disciplines regularly employ specific teaching methods and rely on traditional classroom techniques. Introduction of a new paradigm of classroom interaction, the introduction of technology, and the shift from teacher-centered instruction to student-centered learning are challenges for the faculty and those who are responsible for professional development activities. Recent writings about active learning and participation in classrooms and training venues are now encouraging faculty to shift their teaching paradigm and introduce these concepts into their classroom (Halpern & Associates, 1994; Meyers & Jones, 1993; Silberman, 1996). Since we know from research that adults are likely to learn more and in more complex ways when they are active in their learning (Brookfield, 1986; Lawler, 1991), it is useful not only to teach this concept, but to use it directly in faculty development programs. This active participation provides opportunities for the faculty to integrate their personal and professional life experiences with their new learnings.

This integration is important for the adult learner, who seeks application of new learning to the world around them. Adults seek to make meaning of their learnings, both formal and informal, as they proceed through life (Bee, 1996; Brookfield, 1986; Taylor & Marineau, 1995). As we learn more about the unique faculty we serve as professional developers, we can see how to make these connections and to incorporate concrete strategies, which the faculty can readily utilize in their professional work. Knowles (1989) urges us to acknowledge that "adults are life-centered (or task-centered or problem-centered) in their orientation to learning" (p. 84). While adult learners may be interested in this immediate application of learning to the world around them, they may also be interested in the development of self-awareness and self-insight (Brookfield, 1986). Life-centeredness and the attempts to make meaning of learning and expand self-awareness are pivotal points upon which to create and deliver professional development programs. Educators of adults encourage reflection on practice for professionals and suggest classroom practices to facilitate this professional expertise (Brookfield, 1990, 1995; Schön, 1983). This process can provide individuals with a more complex, yet intuitive experience of problem solving. Engaging this process is both beneficial for the faculty developer, as well as for the participants in the development activity (Brookfield, 1995; Cranton, 1996).

Finally, we want to consider the importance of understanding how adults differ from children and youth in their learning and how adult motivations and experiences impact learning (Lawler, 1991). We change, grow, and experience the world in different ways as we go through adulthood. These experiences provide diversity among us, in our educational backgrounds, our personalities, and our values and goals. We come to educational events with "baggage" from previous learning, our individual learning styles, and our unique expectations and perceptions. Learning in adulthood is seen not as a compulsory preparation for the future, as it is with children, but as an opportunity to seek understanding of the world around us and the changes inherent in our adult life (Apps, 1991). As we seek out useful and effective strategies for working with adult learners, these concepts offer a distinct and different perspective for creating professional development programs for faculty on our campuses.

Principles of Adult Learning

These fundamental concepts from the literature provide a foundation upon which we can apply principles for faculty development initiatives (Lawler, 1991). Utilizing the wealth of literature and research, we can articulate six adult learning principles to guide us in our faculty development programming:

1. Create a climate of respect.

2. Encourage active participation.

3. Build on experience.

4. Employ collaborate inquiry.

5. Learn for action.

6. Empower participants.

The adult learning principles will serve to inform faculty development with the literature and practice of adult education.

First, it is crucial to **create a climate of respect** for adult learners. Grounded in humanistic philosophy and sound organizational theory (Elias & Merriam, 1995; Galbraith, 1998), this perspective encourages us to start where the learner is by taking into consideration from the beginning the characteristics, values, and educational goals a learner brings to the education event. In creating a respectful climate, we seek out an environment for learning that provides participants with both a physical climate and a social climate conducive to adult learning. This requires us to take into consideration the characteristics of our learners, their learning styles, their academic and educational training, and in particular with faculty, an understanding of their unique professional perspective.

In doing this we **encourage active participation** in the learning event from its conception to the evaluative and utilization phase. Adults are accustomed to being active participants in their daily lives. Faculty continually make decisions regarding curriculum content, assess student learning, and research new ideas in their discipline as they go about their professional duties on campus. Being respectful of their professional expertise by inviting participation and collaboration encourages learning. Lawler (1991) suggests that "Adults learn more effectively and efficiently when they actively participate in the educational activity" (p. 39). A learning climate that encourages and facilitates this active interchange involves the faculty in all stages of programming and in particular in the seminar or workshop delivery. This will also create goodwill and a cooperative environment.

An active learning environment presupposes the value of the faculty's experience. Adults come to education with a wealth of experience, and faculty with their academic training are no exception. This experience provides a rich resource for program development and the actual learning itself. This fundamental principle, "adult education includes and **builds on the experience** of the participant" (Lawler, 1991, p. 61), is useful for the faculty developer. We cannot divorce the learner's past experience from the present educational event. Instead, we should be using it as a springboard for new learning and active participation in the professional development initiative. An important aspect of this experience is its diversity. Adults will bring their worldviews based on their personal histories with them to the learning event (Apps, 1991). These will influence the acceptance of information and affect how learning occurs. We do well to consider this expertise and seek out opportunities to use it. As we will see in the following chapters, engaging the faculty and tapping their experiences are crucial for success.

Building upon fundamental principles leads us to consider **employing collaborative inquiry.** Learning does not occur in a vacuum, and faculty developers have an advantageous opportunity to include their learners, the faculty, in the many phases of program development, thus acknowledging faculty experience and expertise. Collaboration can be accomplished by involving participants in assessing needs, utilizing small groups in classrooms, and alternating education roles in establishing objectives and goals (Brookfield, 1986). This collaborative mode of inquiry requires that all involved with the educational event participate in the various tasks in planning and delivery. It is useful to consider how this collaboration is similar to the familiar concept of collegiality in academic institutions.

Finally, there are two additional principles which adult educators find useful in working with adult learners: **learning for action** and **empowering the participants** (Merriam & Caffarella, 1999). As we construct our faculty development initiatives, we are interested in goals, objectives, and outcomes. Most education involves change, and faculty development usually centers on motivating faculty to consider, implement, and promote new ideas, instructional processes, and learning paradigms. The initiative should be designed with application in mind. Incorporating the concept that learners will take action on their learning and will utilize the information presented after reflection is crucial for change to take place (Cranton, 1997; Mezirow & Associates, 1990). Activities should include a supportive environment in which experimentation can take place along with the identification of options for application. When learners are able not only to comprehend new information but also to place it in their context, make meaning of it, and take action to incorporate it into their daily lives, they become empowered (Cranton, 1997).

A goal of adult education is change and growth. It is a central rallying point that we value the belief that adults can grow and change throughout their lifespan. As we see the faculty as autonomous individuals able to change, we incorporate strategies to empower them in their professional lives. This perspective is based on the belief that adults are capable of understanding their range of possibilities with the ability to make choices based on this awareness and understanding (Brookfield, 1986). Being able to influence and change one's environment as a result of an educational experience leads to empowerment. A sense of empowerment leads to action, not only in the individual classroom, but also throughout the institution. Professional development activities are usually created to solve a problem and initiate change within both learners and the organization in which they work. Having empowerment as a fundamental principle of faculty development underlying the development and delivery of these activities is a step toward realizing these goals. These fundamental principles can guide us in a more thoughtful process of creating professional development activities. Now we can turn to the adult education program planning literature and its contribution to the Adult Learning Faculty Development Model.

Program Planning

Adult education has contributed greatly to the progress of program development theory and practice. Books and articles abound, providing the practitioner with useful models, strategies based on sound programming principles, and adult learning concepts (Caffarella, 1994; Cervero & Wilson, 1994; Cookson, 1998; Knowles, 1980; Sork, 1991). In assessing this abundant theoretical literature and practice, we have distilled important concepts and ideas to facilitate the process of faculty development. Taking the crucial ideas and incorporating them into the model for faculty development provide a foundation for effective faculty development. We have identified five basic program planning concepts from the field of adult education that are integral to faculty development. Effective program development is:

1. Nonlinear

2. Contextual

3. Evaluative

4. Fundamental

5. Responsible

Early writings in curriculum and program development (Boyle, 1981; Tyler, 1949) depicted the process as linear with a series of steps to be accomplished in an additive progression. Many of these models for programming isolated the process and depicted developers in a mechanical mode working their way incrementally through each step. Theorists and practitioners now see the benefits of approaching program planning as a **nonlinear**, intricate, and fluid process (Caffarella, 1994; Kowalski, 1988; Murk & Galbraith, 1986; Murk & Walls, 1997; Sork & Buskey, 1986). We concur, and propose that it is essential for effective faculty development to see planning as complex and ongoing. Such a perspective recognizes that program planning does not proceed in a simple sequenced step-by-step process, but instead elements of each stage are closely linked and may overlap. A nonlinear model is much more consistent with the practitioner's experience and therefore is more helpful for application.

The second concept that emerges from the literature proposes that adult education program planning cannot be done in a vacuum. In order to be effective and succeed, program planners need to be cognizant of the social, political, and organizational **context** (Cervero & Wilson, 1994, 1996; Kozlowski, 1995; Mills, Cervero, Langone, & Wilson, 1995; Wilson & Cervero, 1997). Experienced planners recognize that a good program is not enough. In order to be effective, the program also needs to be consistent with organizational goals, couched within the organizational culture, and accepted by organizational political powers. While this may sound like the corporate world to some, the literature and practical experience make it clear that this is also the same situation in formal educational institutions (Birnbaum, 1988; Caffarella, 1994; Wilson & Cervero, 1997).

A comprehensive **evaluative** theme is the third concept that adult education program planners contribute to faculty development. While frequent practice may be to equate evaluation with standard objective post-workshop rating forms or "smile sheets," quality program planning sees evaluation as a theme that runs throughout all aspects of the program planning (Caffarella, 1988; Chen, 1990; Knowles, 1980; Posavac & Carey, 1992). The formative aspect of evaluation occurs at the beginning of the planning process while the methods of evaluation are chosen for a program. It should be continually employed as the program is underway to enable implementation of necessary changes. Finally, summative evaluation is the reflective assessment of participants at the end of a program. To use only summative evaluation, which may be common practice in many professional development venues, is to deny the program planner the opportunity to improve a program in progress. Continuous evaluation is essential for effective planning (Lewis & Smith, 1994; Posavac & Carey, 1992).

Getting the total picture of the planning process is significant for the faculty developer. This picture includes all the **fundamentals** necessary for the program which include: needs assessment, program and learning objectives, delivery, evaluation, and follow-up (Caffarella, 1994; Knowles, 1980; Knox, 1986; Sork, 1991). These fundamental elements are continually enumerated in the literature and provide a systematic approach to getting the job done. They offer a general basis from which to build all programs and a conceptual framework with which to organize the task inherent in the process.

Finally, the necessity of **responsible** program planning is a critical concept to be considered in this overview. Ethically and socially responsible considerations cannot be separated from effective adult education program planning. Faculty developers need to be aware of their obligations as program planners. These would include their role responsibilities and the perspectives they take on participants' rights during not only the actual program, but throughout the entire planning process. Recognizing ethical dilemmas and the political dimensions of planning within organizations is crucial for success. These issues have been discussed in the literature and serve to guide adult education program planning through many different circumstances and questions (Brockett, 1988; Cervero & Wilson, 1994; Galbraith, Sisco, & Guglielmino, 1997; Imel, 1991; Lawler, 1998; Sork, 1988; Uhland, 1994). The lessons that are indicated from this continually developing theme should be fully integrated into all adult education program planning.

These five concepts represent the overarching themes of program planning in adult education: a nonlinear approach, organizational context, evaluation, inclusion of fundamental elements, and responsible planning. They form a firm base of theory, research, and practice upon which to build faculty development efforts.

The Adult Learning Model for Faculty Development encompasses these adult learning and program planning principles. By building on this rich foundation, the model has a deeper foundation and potentially greater outcomes. As we discussed, faculty development gained emphasis in the 1970s. Adult learning principles were brought to the forefront in the 1980s and 1990s. Now, we bring the two together for the benefit of more effective faculty development programs. The Adult Learning Model for Faculty Development casts faculty development under the scope of adult learning, and thereby enables faculty development initiatives to benefit from the discipline by understanding the adult learner.

THE ADULT LEARNING MODEL FOR FACULTY DEVELOPMENT

It is a Thursday afternoon in early January. Sharon McCarthy, the chair of the Faculty Development Committee at Norris Community College, convenes her first meeting of those interested in conducting a professional development seminar for the college's faculty scheduled for the end of the spring term. As people gather in the meeting room, many diverse and specific expectations for the seminar are voiced. People begin to talk about the many possible topics that could be covered, and the noted experts who could be invited to speak. Ideas are suggested at a hectic pace, yet no systematic direction for planning this endeavor emerges. Sharon had hoped that one person would emerge as the leader of the group, but instead it is apparent to her that there are several constituencies represented who are only interested in their individual perspectives. As time draws the meeting to a close, the group has compiled a long list of prospective topics and speakers for the seminar. Sharon, overwhelmed by the creative brainstorming that had taken place, is also frustrated and unsure about what to do next.

Our story highlights some of the real issues that those responsible for initiating faculty development programs encounter, and where a more systematic, thoughtful approach is needed. We believe that if Sharon had used a systematic model, the work of planning for faculty development would have gone much more smoothly. Let us visit again with Sharon as she adopts the Adult Learning Model for Faculty Development.

Sharon McCarthy has invited each department in the college to send a representative to a faculty development planning session. These representatives have been asked to prepare a list of topics that they and their colleagues would be interested in having faculty development initiatives focus on and to identify dates and times that the faculty would be available to attend a workshop next semester. As the group convenes, Sharon distributes a checklist for the Pre-planning Stage of faculty development programming. This enables the participants to follow along during the meeting and to give them an overview of this step. The information that the participants have brought with them is collected and tabulated on two white boards in the room. Once every-one is introduced, Sharon directs the discussion to the goals and objectives of faculty development as framed in the mis-sion and goals of the college. From this basis, the group begins to discuss the list of faculty development topics sug-gested by the faculty.

This new scenario has a very different beginning than the original scenario. Sharon is able to gather a representative group of faculty members who clearly have the needs and concerns of the faculty in mind. Additionally, she has invited the partici-pants to begin a systematic plan; they know what is in store for this first stage and their views are valued. By using a model such as the Adult Learning Model for Faculty Development and its associated checklist, individuals and committees can approach the task in an organized manner with the needs of the faculty, the adult learners, clearly in mind.

The Model

Based on our experience, research, and understanding of the principles of adult learning and program planning, we have developed an inclusive conceptual model that brings together the many tasks included in programming for faculty development. The framework is illustrated in Figure 2.1.

This framework depicts adult learning principles and adult education program planning principles as the "tracks" upon which the stages of a faculty development program travel and progress. Without the support and direction provided by the framework, the process of faculty development will be misdi-rected. Figure 2.2 further explains the model by illustrating the

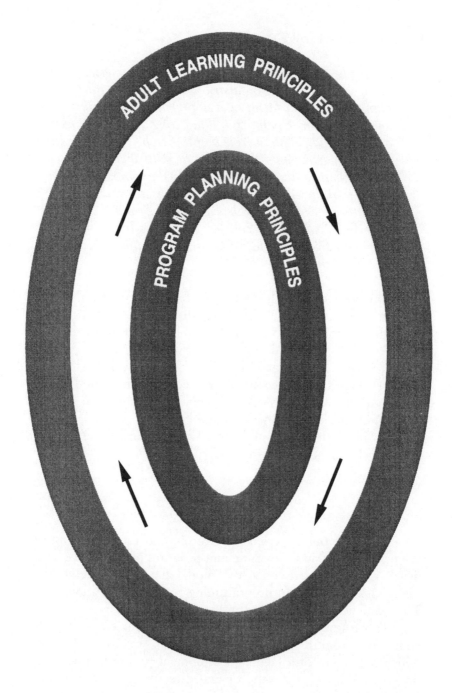

Figure 2.1 The framework of the Adult Learning Model for Faculty
Development

four stages: Preplanning, Planning, Delivery, and Follow-up and their interactive relationships to the framework and to one another.

The model conceptualizes planning faculty development both specifically and holistically. It becomes a guide from which to view the needs and issues that face faculty developers. Theory and practice are combined. Adult learning principles and program planning principles are incorporated into each stage. To try to do faculty development effectively without the benefit of the literature and practice of either one is to try to drive a train on only one rail. It would be a series of false starts that would result in a wobbly and precipitous ride.

Another feature of this model is the interrelationship of the stages. As depicted in Figures 2.2 and 2.3, the faculty development process is modeled as a closed loop that is not solely linear. Instead, it is a dynamic model that includes movement and progress as it follows a course. The issues that are dealt with in one stage very often arise again at other stages. For example, evaluation is not delegated solely to the Follow-up Stage; instead it is considered and planned for even in the Preplanning Stage and again in each successive stage. The themes and issues are connected and represented throughout, and the path of the model allows for movement between the stages as well. For example, in the Planning Stage the developer must return to information, such as needs assessments, done during the previous Preplanning Stage. There is an articulation, a fluid, dynamic movement among all stages in this model.

Another important complementing feature of the model is that it fundamentally incorporates interrelated and common themes throughout. Such themes include adult learning principles, program planning principles, and the guidelines developed in this book. These are not principles to be considered only once in planning faculty development, but are to be returned to again and again throughout the process.

The ultimate goal of the model is to act as a guide for the faculty developer in building programs that will meet the academic and professional needs of faculty. Using it in this manner emphasizes greater empowerment of the faculty as adult learners

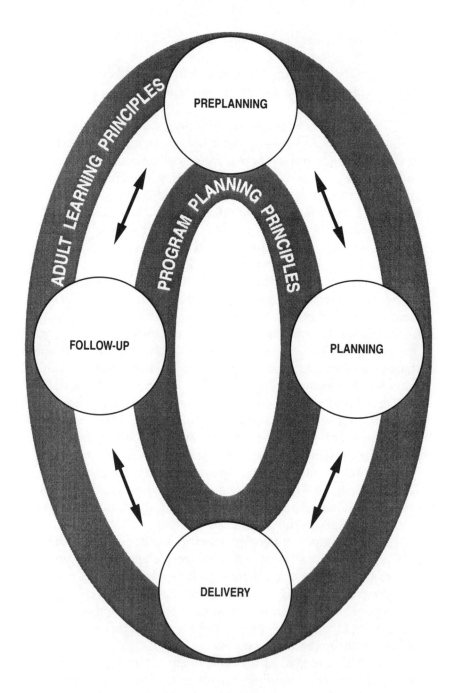

Figure 2.2 The stages of the Adult Learning Model for Faculty Development

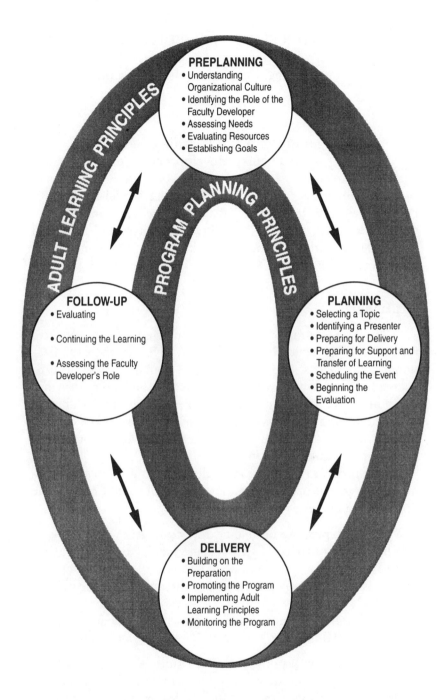

Figure 2.3   The stages and tasks of the Adult Learning Model for Faculty
Development

throughout the planning, the program itself, and the follow-up activities.

Stages of the Adult Learning Model for Faculty Development

The four stages of the Adult Learning Model for Faculty Development are Preplanning, Planning, Delivery, and Follow-up. Each of these stages will be introduced here and presented in full detail with its associated tasks, issues, and concerns in Chapters 3 through 6.

Preplanning

The Preplanning Stage is the beginning point for effective faculty development. Here attention is given to the organizational goals, needs, and organizational climate. These need to be assessed and investigated to prepare for the faculty development initiative. Adult learning principles also need to be applied from the beginning. This stage will use the lens of the organization and the faculty, the adult learner, to provide an organized starting point and direction.

The program planning and adult learning interests in faculty development may be formulated into four questions for the Preplanning Stage:

- What is the purpose of faculty development?
- What is the purpose of this specific faculty development initiative?
- How is faculty development tied to the mission of the institution?
- What resources are available to support a faculty development initiative at this time?

These questions will guide our discussion as we seek to lay a solid groundwork for faculty development activities. In Chapter 3, these questions will encompass a series of tasks that the faculty developer can follow. Preplanning provides a beginning point for the faculty developer and introduces the perspectives of regarding the faculty as adult learners and assessing organizational goals.

Planning

Preplanning determines the overall direction of faculty development, whereas the Planning Stage involves structured preparation for what specifically will happen during faculty development initiatives. The questions to be answered in this stage are:

- What will happen during this faculty development initiative?
- Who will be involved—faculty, developers, and presenters?
- How will we organize the effort—support, deliver, schedule, and market?

At this point, faculty development will be engaging and supporting the faculty, determining a topic, identifying a presenter, preparing for the program delivery, designing for support and the transfer of learning, and addressing scheduling and evaluation needs. Adult learning principles that are critical in this stage are: creating a climate of respect, building on the faculty's relevant professional experience, planning for active participation, learning for action, and empowerment. Employing these principles in the early stages of faculty development programs can have many positive effects by building genuine goodwill, ownership, and excitement for what is to come. These elements cannot be taken for granted. They are important components of success, and worth the effort and time taken to develop them. The purpose of the Planning Stage is to give a comprehensive structure to the myriad of preparations.

Chapter 4 offers a complete look at the tasks and issues of the Planning Stage. This discussion and the associated tasks will offer substantial direction for the faculty developer in systematically approaching faculty development and cultivating support for such programs within the organization.

Delivery

The tasks, issues, and concerns surrounding the actual faculty development programming are presented in the Delivery Stage. The purpose of the stage is to produce a program that will achieve the goals established for the program and ensure the desired outcomes for both the faculty and the organization. The Delivery Stage offers the opportunity to fully integrate adult learning principles into the substance of the program through using active and collaborative learning techniques, addressing the needs of the faculty, and emphasizing application of learning.

As the Delivery Stage begins, four questions should be addressed:

- Are we continuing to build on our preparation?
- How do we effectively promote the program?
- How are adult learning principles implemented?
- How do we monitor the program?

The Delivery Stage will also build on the preparations of the previous stages, determine effective ways to promote the program, and engage in formative evaluation. This stage may be seen by some faculty developers as the entirety of faculty development; however, the Adult Learning Model for Faculty Development offers a greater context and impact that reach beyond the individual tasks. Chapter 5 will discuss the Delivery Stage in detail with a complete discussion of the ways in which faculty development can benefit from putting adult learning principles into practice.

Follow-up

Programming for faculty development does not end with the event. Especially since many faculty development programs are ongoing in educational institutions today, it is important to consider what happens after individual events conclude. The Follow-up Stage addresses tasks, issues, and concerns that both the faculty developer and the organization may have in the application of the learning. Support for changes in thinking and behavior, along with consideration of future development activities, is important at this point. It is during this time that the faculty developer sees evaluation as an integral part of the process by using both formative and summative evaluation. This stage also emphasizes supporting faculty in continuous learning and the implementation of learning. The adult learning principles continue the climate of respect, participation, and learning for action. The questions that will be answered in this stage include:

- What is our evaluation plan?
- How will ongoing support be provided for what was learned?
- What can we, as faculty developers, gain from reflecting on our role in this endeavor?

Chapter 6 presents a thorough overview of this stage along with guidelines for faculty developers to reflect on their role. It is also an opportunity to look at the meaning of the program for the individual and the organization with a vision for how future initiatives may build on these efforts. During this stage we are keenly aware of determining how the organizational environment can support new learning and what needs to be done to encourage faculty to implement information and skills learned in their daily practice. The "reflective practitioner" perspective is critical for the success of all the stages, but especially in the Follow-up Stage.

A Third Dimension for the Adult Learning Model for Faculty Development

As we look at the conclusion of a faculty development initiative, a third dimension for the Adult Learning Model for Faculty Development should be considered. As the planning and programming processes unfold, important indications for future faculty development initiatives develop which can be channeled into avenues for future efforts. In addition to identifying these topics and themes for future programs, this is an opportunity for growth. That is, each cycle will bring new observations, wisdom, and guidance to future endeavors. We learn about the specific program to be offered, and we also learn about the planning process itself. This learning can be carried forward to inform the next stage, but even further, it can be carried to the next set of faculty development initiatives.

What have we learned about programming in our institution and with our faculty? What have we learned about faculty as adult learners and education professionals? What have we learned about ourselves as faculty developers and maybe also as administrators or faculty? The reflection characterized in the final stage should be a theme throughout all stages of the model. It will lay the groundwork for future programs and will provide some assurance that we will learn from the past. The next cycle of the model will not just traverse this set of tracks but will build upon the previous cycle and lift us higher in a process of continuous improvement.

In this way the three-dimensional spiral in Figure 2.4 may best characterize the model as it is viewed in the context of faculty development initiatives for an educational institution. The two-dimensional model helps us look at the program at hand; the spiral lets us look at our place in time, history, and improvement. In the latter model, the three-dimensional disks represent the Adult Learning Model for Faculty Development and the large arrows indicate reflection and time leading to future faculty development initiatives.

SUMMARY

In this chapter, we have presented and explained the Adult Learning Model for Faculty Development which is based on the integration of the fields of adult education and program planning. The principles of these fields are the supporting framework of a model that goes beyond traditional faculty development initiatives. By looking at faculty as adult learners,

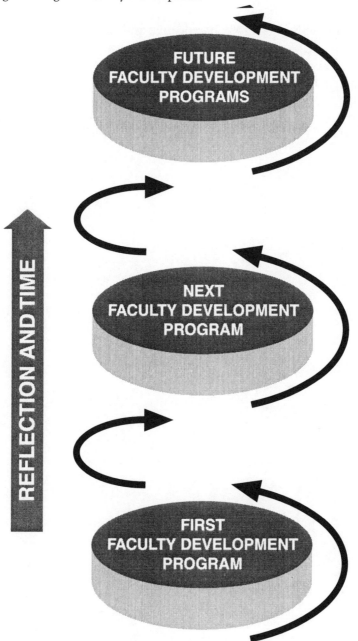

Figure 2.4   A third dimension of the Adult Learning Model for Faculty
Development

this model brings a new perspective and strategy to faculty development.

The four stages of the model provide a specific direction that leads us through successful programs. These individual stages are discussed in depth in each of the next four chapters. The focus will be on the practical issues and concerns of the stages and the tasks that need to be accomplished.

CHAPTER 3

Preplanning

Mary Jenkins, director of special programs at Walburn College, was enthusiastic upon returning from her annual professional meeting. Many discussions had centered on faculty development programs, and the keynote speaker had focused on the importance of teaching and learning centers that were becoming more prevalent and influential on university campuses throughout the country. She was ready to bring this message back to her campus and thought a miniconference for faculty would be the perfect way to start. Back in her office Mary invited several faculty and staff across the campus to discuss this initiative. At their first meeting, there was much brainstorming, famous people were considered for keynote speakers, a conference hotel was suggested, themes and topics were recommended. Each person was eager to share a vision of how the mini-conference should be organized and what topics it should focus on. Six months later this group was still meeting and brainstorming. Word was out on campus that faculty development was in the works, but there was little enthusiasm among Walburn faculty since nothing had materialized. Mary was now frustrated but unsure how to proceed. Her committee kept coming up with good ideas, but ones that were not realistic for Walburn, especially when it came to funds available to support the committee's ideas. Mary wondered if she should have proceeded in a different way.

INTRODUCTION TO THE
PREPLANNING STAGE

It is natural to begin planning for faculty development with concrete tasks, such as the identification of a speaker, facilities, audience, and topics. These are all-important considerations. Planning usually begins with to-do lists, discussions among those responsible, and identification of logistical considerations. As we can see from the scenario, Mary was able to get these discussions started and elicit verbal support for her idea of a miniconference. However, she and her committee were not able to get the project off the ground. Anxious and excited to get under way, Mary moved quickly into an action mode to get the job done. This is a common error of planners. We propose that before planning takes place, faculty developers should pose and answer several overarching questions. Inherent in these questions is a series of preplanning tasks and issues to get the developer started in a systematic and thoughtful way. These questions will inform the entire faculty development process and provide a solid foundation for programming. The important questions to ask at the Preplanning Stage are:

- What is the purpose of faculty development?
- What is the purpose of this specific faculty development initiative?
- How is faculty development tied to the mission of the institution?
- What resources are available to support a faculty development initiative at this time?

Preplanning is the beginning point for effective faculty development. Here the goals, needs, and organizational climate are observed and investigated to set the stage. It is a reflective period in which developers should take a holistic approach. This reflective foundation will serve as a guide throughout the entire process. The Preplanning Stage sets the direction for the program and begins the assessment of faculty and organizational needs. Planners can use this stage as an opportunity to understand and define their role as faculty developers and reflect on their practice within their organization. Here, too, is where we begin to see faculty development as an adult learning activity, an activity that starts where the participants are in their learning needs.

In this chapter we will explore how to get started on a faculty development initiative using the five preplanning tasks identified in the model. First, we will take a look at the applicable adult learning principles, which provide a foundation for this stage. Then we will review the tasks. Issues surrounding these tasks and the context of preplanning will be addressed and strategies for applications will be offered.

ADULT LEARNING PRINCIPLES

As we begin to review the tasks and issues of the Preplanning Stage, several principles from the adult learning literature are applicable and helpful. Chapter 2 outlined the principles of adult learning which have been reported in the literature and that we are recommending as a foundation for faculty development. As we consider the questions in the Preplanning Stage, several of these principles apply.

First, if we view the faculty as adult learners, we then can rely on a wealth of information regarding adult learners, including their own experiences, to inform our practice of faculty development. As we ask our questions we begin to acknowledge faculty, their characteristics, and their experiences. The literature tells us that "each person has learning needs, and brings knowledge and resources to the learning process" (Brew, 1995, p. 15). This requires us to consider the faculty's learning needs, not only as perceived by the organization and the developer, but as they themselves perceive their own needs. All constituents need to be considered, but the faculty's voice is required for success here.

One of the most consistent ideas in adult learning is the concept that adults bring a wealth of experience to educational events. Here the faculty will bring not only their experiences as learners but also their experiences as practitioners in the profession of education. These experiences will impact both how they perceive the faculty development event and how they will learn. Knowles brought this to our attention when he formulated his assumptions of andragogy regarding how adults learned. He suggests that "As people grow and develop they accumulate an increasing reservoir of experience that becomes an increasingly rich resource for learning—for themselves and for others" (Knowles, 1980, p. 44). Faculty experience will impact the assessment of needs, the construction of curriculum, the learning process itself as well as the final outcome—the learning goals and objectives of the program. **Building on the experience of the participants** is one of the primary principles of adult learning which help us preplan.

Much has also been written regarding the idea that adults have, as Knowles (1989) labeled it, a "readiness to learn." This readiness to learn is evident when adults experience learning needs in their professional and personal lives (Brookfield, 1986; Taylor & Marineau, 1995). These needs push adults to seek learning opportunities. It may be as simple as getting a new computer and learning the new word processing system or as complex as entering a profession and learning the new roles and responsibilities. Faculty are a good judge of what they need to learn because they are proficient in doing this for the success of their job. Trained as researchers in graduate school, faculty seek to learn new things in their discipline to improve their work in research and teaching.

Connected to readiness to learn is the concept that adult learners are interested in immediate application of their learning (Knowles, 1989; Lawler, 1991). In recent years, the literature of learning in the workplace has helped us understand the importance of applicability and immediacy for the adult learner. "We now recognize that formal learning is effective when people know that they need to learn, experts can provide answers, and practice is relevant to real-life application" (Watkins & Marsick, 1993, p. 25). **Learning for action** requires that at the very beginning we have practical and immediate applications in mind. As professors consider attending a faculty development program, they seek to know just how this information can help them in their work. If we recognize this, we can reconceptualize ideas regarding motivation. Developers also can utilize these ideas to make more sense of what they are trying to accomplish and make clear to faculty what the goals and objectives are.

The principles of adult learning require us to start with the participants, considering their needs and experiences. This perspective encourages us to be thorough in our understanding of both the faculty and the culture of their profession. This openness and willingness to explore this culture and incorporate this understanding into the planning **create a climate of respect.**

Along with the principles of adult learning, several other concepts are useful in preparing and delivering programs for faculty. Foremost is Donald Schön's (1983) concept of the reflective practitioner. He identified reflective practitioners as those professionals who think about what they are doing as they are doing it. This "reflection-in-action" provides the practitioner with a more complex, yet intuitive experience of the problem-solving process. Brookfield early on stressed the importance of Shön's work for program planning, itself a problem-solving process. "There can be few professional fields in which practitioners are required to be so consistently innovative and adaptive; but . . . the professional literature dealing with program development is generally loath to acknowledge the contextually and individual creativity endemic to the process of reflection-in-action" (Brookfield, 1986, p. 248).

We agree with Schön and Brookfield that reflection has importance for faculty developers as they plan. In his later work, Brookfield (1995) emphasizes the importance of "critical reflection," a process of critiquing our assumptions and understanding our actions on a deeper level. He believes that "becoming critically reflective increases the probability that we will take informed actions . . . that can be explained and justified to ourselves and others" (p. 22). This learning should be a basis for practice as Cranton (1996) states, "We can integrate our learning into our practice—learn about teaching while we are teaching—and reconstruct what we know in addition to acquiring new knowledge" (p. 26). This process also increases democratic trust, provides a rationale for practice and grounds us emotionally in the work we are about to undertake (Cranton, 1994). These are important considerations for the faculty developer who will be working within an organizational context with its political implications for programming. As we consider the tasks in the Preplanning Stage, reflection on practice can provide the practitioner with the ability to work beyond the minutia and consider the larger picture of faculty development as adult learning.

The literature of adult learning offers guidelines and principles to enhance programming. It is critical to view faculty development as an adult learning process, the faculty as adult learners, and the developer as an adult educator.

PREPLANNING TASKS AND ISSUES

In our scenario, the faculty developer, Mary Jenkins, did little preplanning before she brought her committee together. We suggest that Mary first answer the Preplanning Stage questions and then consider each of the five tasks. This will provide a foundation for the other three stages of faculty development based on the resources available from the disciplines of adult learning and adult education program planning. The five Preplanning Stage tasks are:

- Understanding organizational culture
- Identifying the role of the faculty developer
- Assessing needs
- Evaluating resources
- Establishing goals

These tasks will be described along with an elaboration of the issues inherent in each.

Understanding Organizational Culture

Just as a fish is the last to "discover" it is living in the environment of water, many of us in colleges and universities are the last to recognize and reflect on the cultural environment in which we work. Cervero and Wilson (1994) strongly urge program planners to recognize and understand the political and practical dimensions of their work. They see that "planning programs is a social activity in which people negotiate personal and organizational interests" (p. 4). They lay out a conceptual framework to aid the planner in recognizing the culture of the organizations, the power dynamics, and their significance. Caffarella (1994) reminds us that we develop programs within an organizational context, not a vacuum. She defines context "as the situational and environmental factors that affect decisions planners make about programs" (p. 45). This is useful in guiding us in what we look for, as we understand our institutions and their motivations in providing programs for faculty development.

Following this expert advice, it is imperative to consider the organizational environment before planning begins. This first task entails scanning the organization for political agendas and power relationships. This can begin with gathering a history of faculty development and its meaning within the institution. As mentioned in Chapter 1, faculty development historically encompassed such venues as sabbaticals, professional conferences, and academic meetings. The goals of these venues were usually connected to the academic discipline of the individual faculty with the goal to enhance scholarship. As the focus of faculty development has changed in recent years across campuses, more and more emphasis has been placed on teaching and learning in the classroom and meeting the challenges of student diversity and technological advancements (Cox, 1994–1995). It is important to understand if such changes have occurred on your campus. Exactly how do the faculty view faculty development initiatives, both professional development venues as well as campus programming? This is a crucial question to answer before proceeding. Other history to be obtained includes types of programming that have been offered in the past. Obtaining information from both faculty and administrators on the outcomes of these events and the perceptions of those outcomes can provide useful clues as to what to avoid. For example, the developer needs to determine if the previous events were successful and what if any follow-up supported the faculty in their learning outcomes.

Organizational culture has many dimensions. "Values and beliefs define what is considered to be important, and hence, that to which organizations attend and respond" (Watkins & Marsick, 1993, p. 158). Institutional mission statements, strategic plans, and program goals are good starting places in understanding the culture. The hidden culture, including power relationships, value systems, special interests, and political relationships, is also important. The astute faculty developer will utilize Schön's concept of reflection-in-action by posing questions and critiquing these questions, their answers, and their underlying assumptions. As information is uncovered, a program-planning journal is useful here to keep track of the findings.

Within this context it is also important to understand the motivations for the faculty development initiative. As the developer, it is helpful to establish the initiator, such as an administrator, a group of faculty, or an outside influence, and to understand the timing and purpose of this particular request for faculty development. This is the time to uncover motivations and embedded reasons and to consider them within the organizational culture. Understanding these motivations may provide openings for building a solid base of support (Caffarella, 1994). Enlisting and building this base of support can make a difference in motivating faculty not only to attend and learn, but also to become supporters of future endeavors. Brookfield (1995) reminds us that faculty will more than likely "want those who are organizing or running workshops and other faculty development activities to be an experienced practitioner who understands the dilemmas, pressures and problems" (p. 54) faculty face. He urges faculty developers to strive for consistency and authenticity in their planning efforts.

Finally, it is important to recognize the faculty's unique place within the college environment (Bergquist, 1992). As mentioned in Chapter 1, faculty members are individual entrepreneurs whose careers have been built on autonomy in the classroom. Getting to know the faculty, their issues, concerns, and expertise is useful in understanding them as adult learners, and in developing programs. Besides the environmental scan of who the faculty are and their expertise, it is important from an adult learning perspective to assess their learning needs. This will provide a starting point for programming ideas and curriculum content.

We saw that Mary Jenkins brought together a group of faculty to help her plan. This step was a good choice because using the faculty as resources is helpful and can facilitate their motivation. The literature on adult education program planning recommends the establishment of an advisory committee (Caffarella, 1994; Kowalski, 1988; Teitel, 1994). In the Preplanning Stage an advisory committee can provide information on the organizational culture, gather support for the faculty development initiative, and measure colleague interest and concerns. Before establishing such a committee, it is important to understand the political dimension of who should be involved within the organizational context. Members should be formally invited and meetings should be timely, organized, goal oriented, and no more than an hour. Kowalski (1988) reminds us that the benefit of such groups "is determined by the perceptions of the adult educator who forms the council and the organization which sponsors it" (p. 119).

The organizational climate and political context will provide important information as you identify your role as a faculty developer. Using this information to understand how your role will be perceived by the faculty will help not only in shaping the programming, but also in eliciting the support and participation of the faculty you intend to target.

Identifying the Role of the Faculty Developer

As we saw in our scenario, Mary Jenkins's primary role at Walburn was director of special programs. Her position did not include the charge of faculty development. She saw an opportunity to share new knowledge and information as a result of

her experiences at her annual professional meeting. In her enthusiasm, she acted impulsively. To prevent the pitfalls associated with the old adage, "You cannot be a prophet in your own
land," those of us interested in doing faculty development need
first to reflect on who we are and what we are about to do.
Whether you are designated as a full-time developer or have this
responsibility as one of many in your job description, understanding the role and its responsibilities and obligations is important.

*At Breckenridge College the director of part-time
studies, Michael Beebe, was selected by the vice president
for academic affairs to initiate faculty development on campus. From a senior management point of view, Michael was
a natural to chair the faculty committee and develop programming for the faculty across the university. His academic credentials were in adult learning, he had continually
and regularly done faculty development with his part-time
university college faculty, and he was an upper level administrator who had experience in budgeting, programming,
and marketing. All of these were perceived as important in-
gredients for successful faculty development. However, as
the process began, and Michael called together the committee made up of faculty from across the university, there was
much talk about the appropriateness of his appointment. A
major focus of criticism was that he had never been a full-
time faculty member and classroom teacher. Another criticism was his status as director of part-time studies, which
was not one of the academic units responsible for the traditional education on the campus. Establishing credibility
with the faculty was crucial. Michael, assessing his role as
a faculty developer, did this by meeting with various faculty
groups to elicit their input and explain his role and expertise. He also called upon his friends in the faculty to promote him across the campus. He then established an advisory committee and solicited their support as the experts.
Within this context, he began to create an environment*

where information flowed and a questioning dialogue was encouraged.

This is an opportune time to reflect on your own philosophy of education and your professional training (Apps, 1991; Zinn, 1998). These both will influence your decision making and perspective toward the endeavor. It is useful to explore your values regarding education in general and professional development specifically. Also, consider in what ways your own education has influenced your ideas regarding teaching and learning. Defining your role as a faculty developer also includes reviewing the responsibilities and your expertise in executing them. Finally, this self-reflection should also include an assessment of your connections with various constituents across the campus community. For example, whom will you be able to call upon for expertise and support? This personal assessment should be ongoing throughout the entire endeavor.

Brew (1995) points out that there is no one definition of development for faculty in academic institutions. Developers may be academics concerned with educational development, or they may be administrative staff more concerned with training. Whichever, she notes that "development is often viewed by senior management as a service, not as a scholarly activity. It is often viewed quite separately from and having no links with educational development with its emphasis on teaching and learning" (p. 12). Developers need to be aware of their professional role in the institution and of the ramifications of doing faculty development. Will it be done under the auspices of that role or within its own context? The political dimensions, including gaining faculty support for any and all projects, depend on how the faculty developer is perceived.

Assessing Needs

The adult education literature provides us with an abundant source of information on needs assessment. Much has been written regarding both formal and informal collection of data regarding the needs of learners (Brookfield, 1986; Jarvis, 1995; Knowles, 1980). Scholars and practitioners in the field have laid an impressive foundation for us. Before we begin the task of assessing needs, several issues must be identified, such as the reasons for doing faculty development, the purpose of the programming, which constituents are advocating such an endeavor, and whether we are responding to a crisis situation or involved in a long-range professional development plan. Our first two tasks regarding the organizational culture and our roles as faculty developers will have provided us with many answers and helpful information on which to base this next preplanning task.

As we saw in the first scenario, Mary Jenkins was enthusiastic about her new learning and anxious to share this with colleagues on her campus. Yet, she failed to incorporate her ideas for a faculty development miniconference into the larger contextual picture at Walburn. Although she engaged her committee in discussions on program ideas, she did not consider a more formalized needs assessment approach.

Caffarella (1994) urges us to recognize what we want to accomplish as we begin thinking about program planning. She points out that organizational and individual goals may not coincide. With this in mind, it is helpful to think about planning for faculty development from several points of view. Having elicited historical and organizational background, the next step is to consider all the constituents who will be involved and may be affected by the initiative. Listing them provides a starting point for assessing needs.

If we are to adhere to our adult learning principles, then getting to know and understand the faculty and their needs is imperative. Brookfield (1995) reports that outside experts usually define what a faculty may need; that is, some outsider makes decisions regarding what may be good for faculty with little thought as to what meaning it may have for them. He urges us to be purposeful and organized by "making the 'content' of a faculty development effort teachers' own experiences as learners" (p. 66).

It is valuable to take the time to uncover the faculty's past experiences, their professional needs within the institution, and their personal learning interests. Adult learning theory tells us that adult learners can identify their learning needs, that they are interested in learning information to help them do their jobs, and that they tend to want to learn things that they can put to use in a timely manner. Collecting this information is the next task.

Needs assessment can be both formal, with structured surveys for example, and informal by listening to the various voices across the campus community. Formal processes will require financial and human resources and may take considerable time. Yet, they also provide an opportunity to involve faculty and administration in preplanning. Advisory committee members can provide input. It may be their role to design the needs assessment instrument, or they may be involved in the analysis and validation of the data collected.

Again, thinking of the faculty and their professional culture, we recommend a formal process incorporating a venue in which faculty can provide input regarding their needs and wants. Galbraith, Sisco and Guglielmino (1997) recommend conducting a "need and interest assessment" which applied to faculty development would include gathering data from the faculty and the campus community. This process would also require the planner to examine the prior experiences. The authors go on to identify six common methods that could be used to conduct this need and interest assessment: questionnaires, interviews, observation, standardized tests, group processes, and review of records. Results from these assessment methods can provide a wealth of information, which then will need to be interpreted. As a faculty developer, it is important to reflect on both the concrete data presented in this information and the overall picture which may emerge regarding the concerns the various constituents have about teaching issues on campus. This information should be analyzed within the context of the organization using information from the environmental scan.

Rarely do all constituents report the same needs and interests. The collected data needs to be prioritized, and topics and directions chosen. Cervero and Wilson (1994) remind us that this is a political process. Negotiating power relationships and understanding outcomes of decisions made are critical at this point, " . . . planning is essentially a *social* activity in which people negotiate with each other in answering questions about a program's form, including its purposes, content, audience, and format. . . . programs are constructed by people with multiple interests working in specific institutional contexts that profoundly affect their content and form" (p. 28). The successful faculty developer will take the time to read, reflect on, and use the needs and interest assessment information. This information leads to greater understanding of what faculty want to learn, and what the political and cultural ramifications of programming are.

Having identified the needs of the faculty, it becomes important to review the available and potential resources that are needed to realistically plan a development program that can meet those needs.

Evaluating Resources

An important aspect of support for faculty development is the availability of resources and the constituents who provide these resources. It is imperative for the person responsible for organizing and delivering a faculty development initiative to understand the limitations and accessibility of resources. Mary and her group brainstormed names of many well-known speakers who might come with a high price tag. Without a clear idea of funding, brainstorming may be a futile exercise. Presenters and speakers may require not only a fee, but also preparation, travel, and lodging costs.

Evaluation should include both financial and human resources, including the planner's own time and influence. First, consider the financial resources. The Preplanning Stage is the optimum time to identify and secure funding and create a budget. Sources of funding may be on campus from the budgets of various departments and/or the administration, may come from special faculty grants and institutional support, and may be elicited from outside sources. An added benefit is that funding sources may provide a foundation of motivational support for the project. Administrative support in terms of funds and released time provides an impetus for faculty.

Financial, physical, organizational, and personnel resources must be available for effective programs. Recognizing that the faculty developer and faculty may not have any control over these resources, it should be realized that the lack of them can create difficulties that need to be addressed with the organization. The possibilities for faculty development are largely contingent on available resources from the beginning stages all the way to the final application of the learning. Faculty should have the physical and technical resources to use their learning in a convenient manner. For example, if the institution encourages faculty to learn how to use computer-driven presentations for their classes, then technology should be available in campus classrooms. If faculty members have to order, retrieve, set up, and troubleshoot equipment on their own each week, the necessary support is not being provided. This example of institutional commitment of resources demonstrates the need for both concrete and cultural support.

As funding sources and available monies are identified, a budget should be constructed. It should include all items necessary for the development and delivery of the program. Direct and indirect costs should be calculated. Caffarella (1994) provides a useful model for this process identifying three basic costs: development costs, delivery costs, and evaluation costs. Reviewing all anticipated costs and matching available funds will provide a realistic starting point for planning.

Along with the financial resources, it is necessary to evaluate the human resources. These include sources of ideas, possible presenters, and staff needed to execute the endeavor. On-campus resources such as secretarial support and possible faculty presenters should be considered at this time. As we consider the human resources, we should also be thinking about the political ramifications of using these resources. Cervero and Wilson

(1994) urge organizers to continually reflect on the political dimension of the planning and "to anticipate how power relationships can support or constrain their efforts" (p. 115).

Before moving on to the Planning Stage, there is one more task which is crucial in laying the foundation for successful faculty development. Now is the time to pull all the information we have collected from the organization and its constituents, add our own perceptions and experiences and establish the goals and direction for the faculty development initiative.

Establishing Goals

Stephen Covey (1989) in his book *The Seven Habits of Highly Effective People* urges us to "begin with the end in mind" (p. 98). This is good advice for the faculty developer. As we have seen from the above discussions there are many perspectives, issues, concerns, and constituents that are informing the creation of a program. The role of the faculty developer is to coordinate this information and establish a direction for the program and outcome goals. With the end in mind, we have a benchmark for our decision making and prioritizing. This is also the time to begin thinking about evaluating the initiative. It is important to establish outcome goals as well as the manner in which they will be measured.

One of the problems Mary and her faculty colleagues faced was a lack of direction. Aside from sharing new information, there did not appear to be any purpose to their task of creating a miniconference for Walburn's faculty. Had Mary identified, assessed, and prioritized the needs and interests of the faculty at large, she would have had a foundation for her conference.

As objectives are considered, the developer should also be aware that education programs produce both intended and unintended outcomes (Brookfield, 1986). Very often unintended outcomes are positive experiences, where participants gain new learning in areas not planned for in the development of the program. For instance, as the presenter is demonstrating technology use in the classroom, the participants may also be sharing classroom experiences with technology. Many areas of interest may be covered here that are not planned for and yet are genuine and valuable. The developer may think about unintended outcomes and hope they will happen, but by their very definition they cannot be planned. What can be planned for is a learning environment that encourages independent thinking and exploration and provides opportunities for the faculty to share either during or after the sessions.

This is a good time to write out a directional plan for what we want to accomplish. This can be done by answering questions, such as: What do we want faculty to be able to do when the event is over? What changes do we hope to accomplish with the faculty and within the organization? How will we know we have achieved our goals? After gathering this information and answering these questions, we will be ready to formulate the goals of the faculty development programming. These goals will be useful in developing curriculum, campaigning for support, marketing the program, and evaluating outcomes. All of these important tasks are part of the Adult Learning Model for Faculty Development and will be discussed in the following chapters.

PREPLANNING STAGE AT WORK

A systematic formula for faculty development does not stifle creativity or enthusiasm. It does, however, provide an organized way of approaching a task to ensure that important information will be included in the process. Mary's approach to faculty development was unfocused and haphazard. Yet she was very anxious to create a meaningful activity for the faculty at Walburn. Perhaps had Mary first asked the four Preplanning Stage questions she might have had more of an opportunity for success:

- What is the purpose of faculty development?
- What is the purpose of this specific faculty development initiative?

- How is faculty development tied to the mission of the institution?
- What resources are available for the faculty development initiative at this time?

First, Mary would begin to understand her own motivations for doing faculty development and whether or not they fit in with the mission of Walburn. Then she could go on to enlist her faculty colleagues and begin to collect information on the institution, its history of faculty development, and the culture in which it occurs. For instance, Mary may find that there have been several attempts at faculty development in the past, all with little or no success. She then can uncover reasons for these failures, whether they were the results of poor timing, lack of interest, inappropriate topics, or inadequate promotion. She can also review the political climate and whether the faculty were involved in the process. Most important, she can attempt to uncover whether or not the past events were attempts at fixing problem situations. This is the opportunity for Mary to learn from prior mistakes, build on past successes, and become a reflective practitioner.

Mary made a good start by enlisting faculty help. In creating her advisory committee, Mary may now want to put more thought into who is represented on the committee and be more specific about its charge and the work it plans to accomplish. One charge would include the needs assessment. Mary may find in surveying the Walburn faculty that miniconferences were not well attended on campus and that the faculty prefer to learn in short, frequent on-campus workshops. This committee could also help Mary in establishing goals. From here Mary could assess the resources she has available and construct a preliminary budget. This would also be a good time for Mary to create a timeline for getting the initiative off the ground with deadlines for everyone working on the project.

As we saw with Mary, enthusiasm and good will are not enough to get a program initiated. Even before program planning begins, there are critical questions to be asked and tasks to be accomplished.

SUMMARY

The Preplanning Stage of the Adult Learning Model for Faculty Development provides a foundation for the entire process. It includes four questions the faculty developer should pose, answer, and reflect upon, which focus on the reasons for doing faculty development and its connection with the institution's mission and goals. This stage includes five tasks which have been described in detail: understanding organizational culture, identifying the role of the faculty developer, assessing needs, evaluating resources, and establishing goals. These tasks are grounded in adult learning theory and adult education program planning. Each task raises questions and issues, which the faculty developer must address early before beginning the Planning Stage of the model.

CHAPTER 4

Planning

Lee Chang stood outside the auditorium, looking worried and concerned. This was his first year as chair of the Faculty Development Committee and he was watching his first effort go down the tubes. The auditorium was only half full at the beginning of the presentation, and those in attendance were showing signs of leaving. Lee had hoped that this presentation, "Computer Simulations as Medium of Research Inquiry," would be successful since it was being offered in conjunction with Wellsborough College's new strategic plan to encourage research among the senior faculty. For the presentation, Lee had hired a well-known researcher from a corporate-supported research agency based on her reputation and the advice of a colleague at a neighboring research university. Yet, this expert was failing to engage what faculty had gathered in the auditorium. Lee stepped into the room to observe and found that the researcher's delivery was a monotone lecture without participant interaction, and the content focused only on theoretical concerns. As he thought back over his preparations for the event, Lee remembered that he had contacted the chair of the strategic planning committee for ideas on a topic, but had had no other input from faculty across the campus regarding the topic. He also wondered about the poor attendance, since an announcement had been made at the campuswide faculty meeting only a month ago, at the end of the fall semester. No one at that meeting had objected to the presentation being scheduled for the second week of classes at the beginning of this spring term. As Dr. Sharp from the

Psychology Department left the auditorium, Lee asked why he was leaving. Dr. Sharp replied that although the title of the presentation appeared to be relevant to doing research at a small liberal arts college, the content was not, and that during such a busy time, the start of a new semester, his time could be better spent.

INTRODUCTION TO THE PLANNING STAGE

Whether we are new to faculty development like Lee or a seasoned developer, this story holds many important issues that are critical in the early phases of professional development. Building on the foundation set in the Preplanning Stage, developers like Lee can begin a series of tasks that provide a systematic agenda. Early attention to planning will promote effective and successful program delivery. The Planning Stage of the Adult Learning Model for Faculty Development Model maintains a holistic focus on the entire initiative, while covering specific necessary tasks and issues during the preparation. The Planning Stage is guided by adult learning principles, which can influence the success of faculty development programs. During this stage, three questions should be posed:

- What will happen during this faculty development initiative?
- Who will be involved—faculty, developers and presenters?
- How will we organize the effort—support, deliver, schedule, and market?

Each question has related tasks that proceed from the larger context of issues and concerns to be addressed at the Planning Stage. This is a prime opportunity to infuse and benefit faculty development with adult learning principles.

ADULT LEARNING PRINCIPLES

Adult learning principles continue to offer guidance in the Planning Stage. The literature clearly states the importance of preparation for adult learning (Brookfield, 1986; Caffarella, 1994; Knowles, 1980). Examples of such preparation include understanding the needs and experience of the adult learners (Knowles, 1980), involving adult learners in the planning process (Caffarella, 1994), and developing an active learning curriculum (Brookfield, 1986). Planning for adult learning should not be done in isolation from adult learners or their needs and concerns. Each of the adult learning principles outlined in Chapter 2 are actively used in the Planning Stage.

First, the faculty developer needs to look for ways that may encourage a **climate of respect** (Brookfield, 1986; Lawler, 1991) for the faculty participants that will continue throughout planning and delivery. We can begin to achieve this by remembering that the faculty will approach professional development from their specific academic expertise and their experiences in the classroom. As we saw in Chapter 3, faculty should be consulted during the needs assessment design, data gathering, and analysis. Going further to include them in the planning, we can ask them to suggest possible presenters and convenient times to hold the event. The establishment of a faculty development advisory committee offers continued input in such areas. In order to have learner-centered instruction, curriculum development needs to take into consideration the needs, interests, experiences, and capabilities of the faculty who are potential participants. Technically correct content is not enough. Faculty participation in the Planning Stage, with the resultant interest in and ownership of the program, is the key to successful curriculum development and transferable learning.

Additionally, the delivery of the sessions should be planned to **build on faculty experiences in a participative and collaborative mode of learning and inquiry** (Brookfield, 1986; Knowles, 1980; Lawler, 1991). Employing these principles demonstrates one of the major tenets of the Adult Learning Model for Faculty Development: what we know about adult learners should be applied to our professional development efforts with faculty. It is better to plan from the beginning to actively use the faculty's experience in the sessions, rather than finding out at the end that an irrelevant program failed to achieve its goal.

Rather than just exposing the faculty to a broad survey of

new information during faculty development programs, opportunity should be given for the faculty to actively apply what they
are learning. In order for **learning for action** to occur, faculty
must make the connection between their work and the content
of the program. This assumes faculty have been asked to determine their needs in the area under study and to participate
collaboratively in developing solutions that may be applied to
real-life situations (Merriam & Caffarella, 1999). Such consideration during the Planning Stage lays the groundwork for a
program highly relevant to the faculty's needs and concerns.

Additionally, exploring these issues in the Planning Stage
provides specific direction to the presenter about the structure
of the program. Presenters should be aware of the importance
of all of the principles of adult learning as they begin constructing the presentations. Most important here would be **creating a
climate of respect** and **encouraging active participation** during
the program; this will cultivate valuable good will and ownership of the program by faculty. We understand that using these
methods and principles may be more work than the familiar
mode of lecture delivery; however, we believe that the benefits
will more than compensate. Seeing faculty encouraged, excited
and **empowered** by new possibilities for use in their classrooms
is one of the significant rewards of using this approach.

PLANNING TASKS AND ISSUES

Remember Lee Chang's surprise and disappointment at the
outcome of his program for the faculty? This situation illustrates several common problems. First, Lee's timing was poor.
He only made one announcement regarding the event and that
was at a faculty meeting during the last week of a semester when
the faculty were focusing on exams and grading. The event itself
was held just as the new term was starting. Both of these time
frames are among the busiest for the college faculty member,
and any single communication could be easily overlooked. Additionally, publicity of the session was minimal with only a verbal announcement and no reinforcement. Apparently there were

no hard-copy references and no reminder was issued as the time for the program drew near.

Other problems were the inappropriate delivery style of the presenter and the lack of connection between the work of the faculty and the content of the presentation. Lee went on reputation alone and had little interaction with the presenter prior to the event. This resulted in a mismatch between faculty and program and disappointment for Lee at the outcomes of his efforts. Finally, the lack of faculty involvement in the planning was really felt in the poor attendance and lack of interest of the faculty in the topic and curriculum. How could this program have been different? We propose that it could have been different if Lee had followed the Planning Stage from the Adult Learning Model for Faculty Development.

Whereas preplanning determines the overall direction of faculty development, planning sets the stage for what will happen during specific initiatives. Poor planning can lead to the problems described in the scenario, as well as many more. The faculty development initiative may be either a box office hit or a failure, and its success may be determined based on what happens during this, the Planning Stage.

The Planning Stage offers developers the opportunity to strengthen and empower faculty. In many cases, however, a deficit model is communicated instead. Development efforts that are part of a deficit model send a message to the faculty that their educational practice needs to be fixed by outsiders and/or the administration. Programs couched in this perspective discourage faculty cooperation. In many ways, the Planning Stage is an opportunity for the faculty developer and the administration to build a positive climate for faculty development that impacts educational practice. There are six tasks in the Planning Stage:

- Selecting a topic
- Identifying a presenter
- Preparing for delivery
- Preparing for support and transfer of learning
- Scheduling the event
- Beginning the evaluation

Each one of these tasks will be explored in this chapter along with specific issues related to them.

Selecting a Topic

One of the first tasks developers face is to bring the topic of the specific faculty development initiative into focus. The first step is to review the needs assessment completed in the Preplanning Stage. The data collected provides content areas identified as important by the faculty. Seeing their choices of topics included will encourage their ownership of the program. As the results are studied, the different needs have to be prioritized, and decisions made on this account. This is not a sterile, isolated decision; instead, much knowledge concerning the organization and the faculty is embedded in this decision (Cervero & Wilson, 1994).

As the specific content area is developed, plans become more tangible. Many choices will be made on the basis of the focus of this effort. The choice of topic is pivotal in motivating the faculty to take advantage of the professional development opportunity. This is heightened if the topic is identified by the faculty as a need, has a high profile (e.g., technology, diversity), and is action-oriented.

During this process, the topic also needs to be described in terms of program objectives for the faculty development sessions. The emphasis should be action-oriented as it focuses on what the participants will be able to do as a result of their participation (Brookfield, 1990; Caffarella, 1994). For example, to say that faculty development on technology will be conducted is good. However, when faculty are informed that "The participants will learn and practice how to use technology to enhance and facilitate their classroom teaching experiences," specific goals are clearly articulated. An important concern is that the faculty's level of expertise in the session's content area needs to be determined and the session planned accordingly. As an example, if the faculty already know how to create and use basic computer-driven presentations, the focus should be on advanced features and alternative uses of the medium rather than on the rudiments.

In prioritizing the findings of the needs assessment, several concerns need to be considered:

- Which groups of the faculty are reflected in the results?
- What monies will be available for different topics?
- What are current issues for faculty and their students?
- Are there other campus groups who may contribute in some way to a topic?
- What physical resources are available?

Caffarella (1994) provides worksheets to assess these and many other concerns in interpreting a needs assessment. However, even as Caffarella says, this may appear to be an unwieldy process, while the actual process may be more intuitive.

At the same time, it is important here to realize that the raw data of a needs assessment is not the final word in choosing a topic for faculty development. Resources, people, and organizational concerns all need to be considered. We suggest prioritizing the findings of the needs assessment and then aligning them with these concerns. This is an iterative process, as the developer works to coordinate these factors into a focused plan of action. Planning with these concerns in mind will help the program to meet felt needs in a realistic context.

An important concern that emerges from this discussion is that planning choices need to align with organizational concerns and directives (Cervero & Wilson, 1994). For instance, at a university or college where 75 percent of the faculty are tenured and the majority of these faculty are over 55 years of age, a needs assessment may demonstrate interest in programs on retirement planning, financial planning, benefits, and the role of emeritus faculty. However, such topics may not match the administration's goals, which have been adopted for the faculty development initiative—recruitment and retention of new faculty. In cases like this, efforts to serve the tenured faculty may be met with resistance. Their topic choices should not be ignored, but instead addressed and, when necessary, negotiated.

Organizational goals may have a direct effect upon the choice of a focus for specific faculty development initiatives.

Identifying a Presenter

Having identified the content and topic areas, we now move to the second task in the Planning Stage—identifying a presenter. Lee relied on his colleague at the neighboring research university for a recommendation, but did little homework himself on the presenter and her background. We need to consider not only who the experts are on the topic, but whether or not their presentation skills are appropriate, if they are aware of principles of adult learning, and if there will be resources available to support their invitation.

Power issues are inherent in this selection process. Faculty developers should consider several questions which will help them understand these power issues:

• Who will make the decision about which presenter to retain?
• What will be the selection process?
• What credentials and references are required of the presenter?
• How will the presenter be evaluated?
• What area of expertise is needed and at what level?
• Will the presenter be viewed as credible by the faculty?

All of these questions should be addressed with the institution, the prospective participants, and the presenter under consideration in mind.

Another important power issue concerns the political hierarchy, both stated and hidden. The faculty developer does not want to circumvent existing lines of authority or recognized leadership. Scanning the organizational environment, as mentioned in Chapter 3, while considering these questions is imperative. Inasmuch as both the official and unofficial organizational aspects of the institution come into play, the developer should try to maintain the strength of an appropriate fit between the presenter and the program. This may take the form of political maneuvering, and if it is not done this way, even for the purest ideals, the program could lose the support of campus contingents.

In the Preplanning Stage we reviewed resources available for the entire faculty development initiative. Now is the time to look at these resources and see how much can be allotted for the presenter's fee. Careful consideration must be given to all costs involved, not just the stipend, but also travel, accommodations, room rental, presentation equipment, and instructional materials. The availability of the presenter must also be considered. Some presenters may be scheduled months or years ahead of time; others may only conduct programs in limited geographic areas. Another body of information needs to be assessed as well: What are the credentials, expertise, and past performance of the proposed presenter? For instance, there are many examples where notable authors have been asked to speak, and it was later realized that their presentation skills were poor. In light of such experiences, information may be gathered through resumes or curriculum vitas, and references from those who have attended previous sessions.

At the same time that individuals are being identified for programs, the focus should be on the needs of the faculty. For example, Amy may be taking a class at a graduate school of education and think that her professor would be great for other faculty to hear. In this case the process might get reversed and Amy might let the star speaker pick a topic without consideration of the needs of the faculty. Let the focus be needs and goals, not the showcasing of a prominent individual.

Remember that the message is also delivered in the actions of the messenger. The developer needs to focus on the performance of the prospective presenter. Therefore, two related questions need to be asked about the presenter: Does the presenter embody what is being taught? Does the presenter effectively use adult learning principles in his or her work? For example, presenting the benefits and use of collaborative learning techniques in a strictly lecture format should be recognized as contradictory; instead, collaborative group experiences should be demonstrated and used. Since much of the success of faculty development initiatives lies with the delivery of the material and the presentation skills, careful attention needs to be paid to this in the selection process.

A final concern is whether the presenter will tailor the curriculum to the faculty. In some instances, a uniform or canned program may be useful, but in many cases an institutional or departmental needs assessment would have uncovered some specific faculty needs that should be addressed in the sessions. The developer needs to keep in mind that the needs of the faculty are primary in the planning of the program so the program should be directed to them.

Sources of presenters may be close at hand. The campus may offer an abundance of experts in areas of interest. Getting to know in-house resources and becoming familiar with them can be advantageous to the faculty developer. While in some respects it may be that "prophets have no honor in their own land," the developer may stir up ill will by bringing in an outside expert when the faculty has well-recognized and liked experts on the same topic. The faculty is also a rich resource for recommending presenters. Additionally, by consulting the faculty, the developer builds goodwill toward the effort; this will serve as a foundation for cooperation and success.

One way to garner and encourage such involvement is to have an active advisory committee for faculty development. Such a council can be the source of ideas and resources while developing a sense of ownership of the program. This will have great benefits for the faculty developer, the faculty, and the programs. In more than one case, however, resident experts in faculty development, such as those in a school of education, have not been included. This is surely an oversight that the faculty developer cannot afford to make. It makes sense to include talented resources available to us for all aspects of the faculty development program.

As we return to more mundane, yet important matters, the issues of time and money must be faced when selecting a presenter. As has been discussed, the issues regarding scheduling come into play here along with the constraints of institutional budgets. There are also larger questions: Is it prudent to spend a lot of money on a renowned person or is an effective but less famous and less expensive presenter just as good? Should the school work around the presenter's schedule to the detriment of faculty involvement? These are just some of the issues that may need to be addressed in this task of the Planning Stage. Once the presenter is identified, attention turns to how the developer and the presenter will prepare for the program.

Preparing for Delivery

As planning continues, one major distinction of the Adult Learning Model for Faculty Development becomes obvious: the delivery of the faculty development initiative needs to model and incorporate adult learning principles. The developer should work with the presenter to determine which appropriate techniques will incorporate the learners' needs and goals, the session objectives, active learning, reflection, and applied learning. This means that the developer needs to communicate much information about the faculty and the proposed program to the presenter. Faculty development programs are a cooperative venture; if a presenter is not interested in working with the developer, he or she is not the right one for the task.

Additional aspects in this preparation include pre-session activities, action plans, and follow-up. Extending the reach of the program beyond the two-hour session greatly increases the likelihood that the participants will remember and use the content. Often busy faculty members run from meeting to meeting and class to class in an overloaded schedule that allows for little reflection. Building reflection, action plans, and follow-up into the program design will make the effort much more beneficial for all involved. These are all part of the way that a topic is presented. Materials need to be prepared, and the program planned to incorporate these parts.

The curriculum should be planned and developed to incorporate adult learner principles such as learner involvement, a learner-centered focus, application emphasis, and flexibility. Adult learning principles and teaching techniques should be applied at all stages of the program's development. A difficult question is whether the presenter will work with the developer in order to benefit from the developer's knowledge of the faculty and their needs. If the developer wants or needs to continue to be involved in this task, this should be made clear during presenter selection so there will be no surprises for either party as they continue. The organization must also realize and allow for the investment of time involved for both presenter and developer to create a program that will involve these many pieces.

What will best fit the faculty? How can we encourage them to change with the new learning? These are important issues that tailor the delivery of the program to a specific audience with specific needs. Finally, as has been confirmed in the literature several times (Apps, 1991; Halpern & Associates, 1994; Lawler, 1991), the program needs an experiential focus. In what way will the presenter be comfortable and effective doing this? What are some alternatives that may be used? These questions lead us to consider the next task in the Planning Stage which focuses on issues of support and transfer of learning.

Preparing for Support and Transfer of Learning

The goals of most educational programs revolve around learning and its application. For faculty, professional development events have been focusing on teaching effectively, adapting to new student populations, and learning technology. This means that the information and skills presented in a seminar, workshop, or class are hopefully applicable to the faculty's needs and can be utilized in their work. Broad (1997) defines this phenomenon:

> Transfer of learning is the effective and continuing application by learners—to their performance of jobs or other individual, organizational, or community responsibilities—of knowledge and skills gained in learning activities. (p. 2)

Caffarella (1994) stresses the importance of planning for this transfer by assisting learners to make changes. This assistance includes support from various segments of the organization.

She provides several examples of this support: "developing individualized learning plans, providing mentors or peer coaches, starting self-help or support groups, offering organizational development interventions" (p. 116). Broad (1997) also cites the importance of organization climate of the application and use of the learning on the job.

Therefore as faculty development initiatives are planned for, a critically important task is that of assessing the environmental climate for support. If the institution has a positive approach to faculty development and sees it as a vital part of its overall mission, then the climate will be conducive for the faculty to implement new learning. If, however, the organization does not view faculty development as a necessary service, there may be little support in the way of scheduling, room assignments, publicity, and financial resources.

Developers need to determine what resources are available to provide support for faculty before, during, and after the faculty development sessions. For example, before and during the sessions, faculty participation may be increased by initiatives to provide coverage for classes, transportation, and compensation if appropriate and needed. After the sessions, faculty will need support to apply their new learning. This may be in the form of people, time, money, and equipment. If the institution does not commit such resources to the faculty, the faculty development efforts may be hindered.

Lack of institutional support and other obstacles need to be addressed. Do the developers have the power to promote an environment that will encourage professional development of the faculty? A scan of the organizational environment can answer this question and may provide alternative courses of action. It must also be assessed whether participation in professional development will benefit the faculty members in their own growth and teaching. For instance, if the new methods learned are used, will this have a positive or negative effect on the untenured faculty's reappointment? For example, if distance learning is not recognized as academically rigorous, uninformed tenured faculty may believe professors involved in it are trying to find the easy way out of teaching. Therefore, in light of reappointment needs, it would not be to the benefit of the new faculty to be involved in distance education development and implementation, and programs on this topic would not likely have much support.

From a broader perspective, being sure that the faculty development efforts align with the mission of the institution will further the efforts. The developer does not want to be at cross-purposes with the institution's message. As in an earlier example, if the emphasis of the school is on new faculty, those efforts that serve new faculty are the ones that will be supported. While this means this is where support will be, it does not mean that the developer should overlook the valid needs of other faculty contingents. Additional rationale and bargaining may be needed, however, before those needs may be represented. We suggest that the faculty developer work with an advisory committee representing faculty and administration to identify, analyze, and prepare to meet the needs of the faculty in the context of the current situation. Such planning can have a proactive effect on available and future faculty resources.

A supportive environment for learning and change will facilitate a transfer of this learning to the faculty's daily work. Much has been written on this concept and its impact on learning in the workplace (Baldwin & Ford, 1988; Broad, 1997; Caffarella, 1994). If one of our goals is application of the learning in the classroom, we certainly want the faculty to use what they learn, not just immediately, but also over the long term. Broad (1997) cites the top three organizational barriers to this transfer: "lack of reinforcement on the job, interference in the work environment and nonsupportive organizational structure" (p. 9). For example, some useful strategies to prepare for transfer of learning are listed in Caffarella (1994):

- Involve key people in the planning process.
- Pretrain supervisors of participants.
- Develop individual learning plans or contracts.
- Use application exercises and simulations.
- Develop support groups.
- Model skills or attitudes/values needed for learning transfer.

- Develop self-monitoring instruments and techniques.
- Involve key players in follow-up activities. (p. 114)

These strategies focus on key players, timing, and organizational considerations that need to be addressed before scheduling the program.

Scheduling the Event

Appropriate scheduling is crucial for program success. Following the principles of adult learning, we begin with the participants foremost in our minds. Faculty work environment and schedules are very different from other members of the university community and must be taken into consideration (Bergquist, 1992). This means programs must fit into the faculty's workload and the pace of the academic year.

Making assumptions regarding faculty schedules can lead to more work and a perception of lack of support.

When Anisa Richardson, dean of arts and sciences, announced in the spring that there would be a fall faculty retreat on professional development, it received a very positive reception and much input from the faculty as to what they hoped to see accomplished during the day's program. No mention of scheduling was made. As she prepared the department's calendar for the fall semester, she selected a date midsemester and entered it on the calendar. As soon as the calendar was distributed to faculty in late August, Anisa began to receive calls from the faculty. One faculty member was to deliver a paper at a yearly conference, another faculty was teaching two classes on that day, one other faculty member was scheduled for another professional development activity, and finally she was informed that the event bordered a long weekend and several faculty would not be available. This created a feeling among the faculty that their schedules and important aspects of their work were not considered in this planning.

Conflicting schedules and responsibilities need to be explored to determine if there is a pattern of availability, or a suggested course of action to relieve some of the conflicts. The faculty advisory committee should be able to identify the heaviest times of faculty workload and help avoid a scheduling disaster like the one Lee Chang encountered in an earlier scenario. For example, if all school committees meet twice a month, perhaps one month's agenda could be changed to one committee meeting and one faculty development session, or perhaps a faculty development program could be incorporated into the monthly faculty meeting. While understanding that not everyone can be accommodated, a determined effort should be made to accommodate most of the faculty.

Including the faculty in the planning means determining what is the appropriate time (morning, afternoon, evening), duration (length of time for session, and the number of sessions), and calendar schedule (beginning, middle, or end of the semester; after the semester). As mentioned in Chapter 1, faculty expect to be autonomous, and their work schedules support this autonomy and independence. Their semesters and days are structured to allow them to complete their responsibilities in the areas of research, teaching, and service, which are different from those of the administration and staff. The faculty also have a distinct culture from that of the rest of a college or university staff, and therefore, the way that faculty development is planned should be different than it is for the rest of the staff (Bergquist, 1992). One might describe the faculty as individuals who are determinedly independent in the midst of a vast hierarchical organization, and this contradiction plays out in many collegiate situations. Getting to know the faculty culture in general and specific to the campus is an important part of scheduling faculty development in alignment with adult learning principles.

Class coverage may need to be arranged for some faculty to be able to participate in faculty development programs. If this is the case, the developer's and/or the dean's office should help to find quality alternatives for the classes. If faculty members are left to fend for themselves in this area, it will become another barrier to their involvement in the program.

The developer may also need to work with the dean of academic affairs in being sure that regular and special scheduled faculty development programs are listed in the faculty's calendars. For example, if faculty development is scheduled before the start of the semester or during break, the faculty should be notified of this well in advance because of vacation schedules, conference schedules, and semester planning. The goal is to complement and not overload faculty schedules.

As we work our way through each of the Planning Stage tasks, it is important to step back and reflect on our progress and how we will measure the success and effectiveness of our efforts. It is not too soon to prepare for how we will evaluate the program and our efforts.

Beginning the Evaluation

The Planning Stage is a good point to start thinking about evaluation, as planning and evaluation go hand in hand (Caffarella, 1994). Evaluation that is built into faculty development right from the start offers more benefits than an evaluation form hastily tagged onto the end of the program. This means creating a plan on how the program will be assessed in reaching its goals and objectives and instilling this plan throughout the entire faculty development process. In other words, the means of evaluating the achievement of the program's objectives are determined and planned at this point. In Lee's case, participating faculty may fill out questionnaires both before and after the program to assess what classroom technology skills they had before and after the sessions. The focus of the evaluation here is on the objectives rather than the process of faculty development. Evaluation data can be critical in improving the effectiveness of programs, but in order to gather that data, plans for evaluation need to start early.

The faculty developer needs to focus on precisely what will be evaluated throughout the program and at its completion, and why the evaluations are being done. The literature encourages us to do both formative, that is ongoing evaluation, and summative evaluation (Brown & Seidner, 1998; Caffarella, 1994;

Wlodkowski, 1993). In Chapter 6, the discussion of the Follow-up Stage reviews the importance of evaluation and its place in the entire faculty development process. For now, we should be identifying the evaluation strategies and incorporating them into our plan.

Formative evaluation throughout the actual program may include such strategies as ongoing reviews, observations, and pilot/field tests (Parrott, 1998). These may be incorporated into the Planning Stage for evaluating how the faculty developer is getting the job done. Parrott (1998) calls this a design review, "an examination of the plans made for the instructional product before the product development begins" (p. 171). Formative evaluation strategies may also be included in the actual program so that program participants can provide feedback on their learning.

Plans also need to include exactly how to collect data at the end of the program. Time needs to be allotted for participant feedback, and instruments need to be designed to capture the information. We are reminded that there are many strategies for collecting summative data that go beyond the standard "smile sheet" we are so familiar with in seminars and workshops (Brookfield, 1986; Brown & Seidner, 1998; Caffarella, 1994). Strategies that are applicable to faculty development include observations, interviews, performance reviews, portfolios and environmental scanning, student achievement, and classroom evaluations. Thinking of evaluation early in program development illustrates the dynamic and cyclical aspects of the Adult Learning Model for Faculty Development. Now let us turn to how this planning could have assisted Lee.

THE PLANNING STAGE AT WORK

The basic elements of keeping a program on track entails a certain amount of planning and Lee Chang certainly had planned and delivered a presentation for the faculty at Wellsborough College. Yet Lee felt that his efforts did not meet his goals and were therefore unsuccessful. This helps us to understand the importance of the concept of planning and all that it encompasses. Had Lee started with a systematic way of developing his program, he might have avoided some of the problems he encountered. We would urge Lee in his next effort to start with our Planning Stage questions and use the tasks as guides in preparation for the event.

- What will happen during this faculty development initiative?
- Who will be involved—faculty, developers, and presenters?
- How will we organize the effort—support, deliver, schedule, and market?

Returning to our opening scenario, how could have Lee used the ideas presented in the Planning Stage to prepare a successful program? First, we would have encouraged him to use a needs assessment to coordinate the organizational goals with the program. This would align the topic of the program with the needs of the faculty and the goals of the strategic plan. Using a needs assessment would have helped Lee to identify those topics of interest and concern to the faculty. The faculty should have voice and power in the choosing of the subject for the sessions. This in itself could have boosted participation and enthusiasm for the initiative.

In addition, organizing support for the efforts should have had a broader base and more direct and positive consequences to reinforce the program's objectives. Examples of support would include released time from classes, adequate equipment resources, and reward incentives that match performance measures within the faculty. Incorporating a strategy for supporting the development efforts before, during, and after the fact will make the experience something with impact on the faculty's professional lives rather than merely a time filler for a two-hour obligatory campus appearance.

Lee's selection of the presenter should have gone beyond hiring an expert in content. Other factors are references, delivery style, and willingness to tailor the presentation to the faculty's needs. Lee could also have worked with the presenter to develop a participatory program addressing issues about which the faculty are concerned. The delivery of the topic may be one of the most significant ways to improve this initiative. Opportunities for the faculty to share their experiences, work collaboratively, and apply their new learning to their professional work should also be incorporated in the program design. Faculty may be surprised and pleased by being sincerely asked to contribute to a truly participatory learning experience (Brookfield, 1990, 1995; Galbraith, 1998). Such learning experiences may include formats such as role play, case studies, simulations, or problem-based learning. This application of learning should be highlighted from the onset in publicity for the session and include time to reflect, develop action plans, and plan follow-up efforts.

Finally, scheduling was a major problem, and hopefully next time Lee would consult faculty, perhaps as an advisory committee, to evaluate faculty and academic schedules for opportune times for publicity and delivery of the program. Avoiding the busy beginning and ending of semesters and providing ample and informative advance notice would have helped. Full disclosure of the content, format, and scheduling of the session should be provided to the faculty well in advance so that they may clearly understand the opportunity offered them and adjust their schedules to include their participation. These changes will help Lee design a successful faculty development program next time.

SUMMARY

The Planning Stage includes six tasks, which lay a foundation for successful faculty development. It begins with three questions to help the faculty developer. The major tasks for the Planning Stage are: selecting a topic, identifying the presenter, preparing for delivery, preparing for support and transfer of learning, scheduling the event, and beginning the evaluation. This chapter has discussed the tasks, issues, concerns, strategies, and guidelines for conducting faculty development programs that will incorporate adult learning principles. Adult learning principles assist in developing a quality effort with many positive effects for the participants, their students, and the college. Particular attention was given to how faculty should be involved in all stages of the planning and participatory action learning. Strategies, including formative evaluation and administrative commitment, also were discussed. With the planning accomplished we are now ready to turn to the actual delivery of the program.

CHAPTER 5

Delivery

The Teaching and Learning Center at Lawking College has been offering workshops and support for faculty development during the last five years. The Faculty Advisory Committee chooses a theme each year as the focus for the workshops. All themes have had teaching excellence as a primary focus. This year the committee has suggested to the director of the center, Rhonda McWilliams, that the faculty across the campus would like to explore how to integrate technology into their classroom teaching and the curriculum. Rhonda planned and offered the first series of hands-on workshops in early spring. One workshop, "The Role of Scholarly Collaboration in Academic Research," was well attended because of the emerging demand for research at the college. However, the evaluations were poor with several faculty expressing disappointment in the workshop since it had not met their expectations. In fact, many of the participants left before the workshop had ended. Rhonda sought out some of her colleagues to see what the problem was. The presenter had focused the workshop on face-to-face, in-residence, extended collaboration and yet had conducted it in a lecture format with little interaction from the participants. Some of the faculty's expectations for the workshop were exploration of online collaboration, practice with technology-based mediums of collaboration, and exposure to collaborative research models. What could Rhonda and the presenter have done differently to change the outcome of this workshop?

INTRODUCTION TO THE DELIVERY STAGE

All of our planning has been leading up to the actual presentation of the faculty development program. Here is where our participants, the faculty, are engaged in learning, and where we can be most effective by using the principles of adult learning. As we saw in our scenario, we cannot abdicate to a presenter our responsibility for effective delivery. We must be aware of how each program will be created and delivered. The Delivery Stage of the Adult Learning Model for Faculty Development includes many critical tasks, specific responsibilities, and principles that will directly impact the outcomes of the actual program. While the Preplanning and Planning Stages incorporated adult learning principles in program preparation, the Delivery Stage offers the opportunity to fully integrate all of these into the substance of the program. Keeping a holistic perspective throughout the entire faculty development process, we continue by posing the questions:

- Are we continuing to build on our preparation?
- How do we effectively promote the program?
- How are adult learning principles implemented?
- How do we monitor the program?

All of the work we have accomplished in preparation for the program provides a foundation for promoting the program and the tools to assess our compatibility with an adult learning perspective. It is now time to implement the various tasks and ideas that we have been planning. Critical to this stage is the continuing assessment of not only program delivery, but also our work as a faculty developer with an adult learning perspective.

ADULT LEARNING PRINCIPLES

This discussion will emphasize the application of adult learning principles to the program's format and describe how the presenter works with the faculty during the actual delivery of the program.

At every stage of the Adult Learning Model for Faculty Development we have been considering the **experiences** of our adult learners, the faculty. These experiences color the faculty's perceptions, expectations, and satisfactions as they participate in a professional development activity. This "baggage" will influence their learning during the event (Apps, 1991; Brookfield, 1995; Cranton, 1996; Knowles, 1980; Lawler, 1991). The experience of faculty in previous faculty development impacts their expectations of the proposed programs. If they have had good experiences, they will be more open and positive concerning the potential benefits of participating in the program. Poor past experiences can certainly stop the faculty from attending an event and may even undermine any faculty development efforts. The environmental scan and the needs assessment can provide information regarding these past experiences.

Another critical factor in the success of the Delivery Stage is that of **creating a climate of respect**. This begins with recognizing faculty experience and letting them know it is recognized and respected. By inviting faculty into the Preplanning and Planning Stages a climate of respect has been initiated, and in the Delivery Stage the developer and presenter need to continue to build a climate that fosters learning, change, and action.

As we have seen in Chapter 4, the faculty's **experience** in their profession is also an important component of delivery. Knowing what the faculty regard as their needs and interests should contribute to determining content and presentation.

Another focus is the **application of the learning**. Research has shown that faculty attending programs are interested in how the information can be implemented (Lawler, DeCosmo & Wilhite, 1996). They are interested in how the learning applies to their own world and work. Faculty developers need to understand this and use it (Wilhite, DeCosmo & Lawler, 1996). When faculty see the relevance of a program to their professional duties and their learning needs, they are more open to program content. This will be evident in positive attitudes, participation, and expectations that will set a successful tone for present and future programs. Promotional materials should clearly describe the relevance and application of the program so faculty will have sufficient information.

The program format also needs to cast subject material in the faculty's context. This may be done in many different ways that incorporate active learning and **collaborative** techniques, such as case studies, case stories, and inquiry-based learning. These methods offer opportunities for faculty to incorporate their own experiences and engage in **active participation** during the program itself. Faculty who leave development sessions with a clear idea of how the content and principles may be put into **action** within their specific settings will rate the sessions highly. Faculty **empowerment** can provide great impetus for grassroots support of faculty development on campus. This is another important dimension where adult learning principles directly impact the success of faculty development programs.

All six of the adult learning principles come into play in the Delivery Stage. What happens as a result of the incorporation of the principles into the Delivery Stage is critical for the success of the current program. It may also lay groundwork for future initiatives.

DELIVERY TASKS AND ISSUES

The faculty who attended the workshop at Lawking College were certainly dissatisfied with the content and presentation. What could Rhonda have done differently to ensure a more positive experience? Our scenario does point toward several shortcomings, that could have been avoided. First, this particular workshop did not fit into the overall goals of the college's faculty development program theme of teaching excellence nor did it address the theme of technology. Second, the session's format and focus were not clearly conveyed to the faculty. Faculty came to the workshop thinking that it would be a hands-on experience and encountered a lecture with little participant involvement. Attending to the tasks for the Delivery Stage could have led Rhonda to a more successful outcome:

- Building on the preparation
- Promoting the program
- Implementing adult learning principles
- Monitoring the program

Building on the Preparation

It is said that many times people lose sight of the forest for the trees, and this may be the case with some faculty development programs. Higher education institutions, faculty development committees, administration, and faculty developers can easily lose focus as they prepare for program activities. In the rush to consider all the details in getting a program off the ground, we can neglect the overall goals, objectives, and direction. At this point, we want to stay focused on the general goals we identified in the Preplanning Stage and assess how they fit with what we are trying to accomplish at this point. We need to go back to the ideas generated in the Preplanning Stage and keep them in mind as we proceed through the Delivery Stage.

As mentioned in Chapter 3, we encourage the faculty developer to act as a reflective practitioner, and here is another opportunity to do so. This reflective exercise, stepping back and looking at the big picture and how each task contributes to it, is appropriate as we begin the Delivery Stage.

First we may reconsider how our specific program fits into the organization. If an institution emphasizes teaching excellence, a teaching excellence theme for faculty development readily fits. In contrast, in such a setting a different focus, such as research, may need to be introduced to and developed with administrators and other key organizational players before it may be effectively adopted. Additionally, if faculty development is seen as an integral function of the organization, allocation of resources will be more readily lobbied for than if it is seen as a peripheral function. Understanding the organization, its structure, and its priorities becomes an important part of grasping the big picture of a faculty development program.

It is also imperative to understand the faculty's needs and

interests. As we saw in Chapter 1, Knowles (1980) demonstrated the connection between learners' needs and learning outcomes. This aspect of control over learning choices is important. In light of this, faculty developers must be constantly aware of the perception that faculty development initiatives have on campus. If they are seen as fixing a problem or as a corrective measure, faculty may feel they have no autonomy and control over their participation in the learning events. Faculty development needs to be seen as a positive endeavor that is part of professional growth and development.

Promoting the Program

A faculty development program can only be effective if faculty participate. This fact places great importance on the task of promoting the program. This includes developing a marketing plan (Galbraith, Sisco & Guglielmino, 1997; Simerly & Associates, 1989), which includes reviewing the program's mission and goals, assessing and targeting the potential audience, and deciding what marketing mix of materials and venues are appropriate and affordable. Promoting a program can start with establishing a reasonable timeline for announcing, informing, preparing, and reminding participants. As mentioned during the discussion about scheduling programs, faculty have schedules that are filled with many commitments and responsibilities that are charted a semester at a time. When faculty development activities are scheduled and announced well in advance, more faculty are able to make room in their schedules for them. Even with this planning, timely reminders are needed.

Publicity materials should be created and distributed (Caffarella, 1994; Kotler & Andreason, 1987; Wilms & Moore, 1987). Caffarella (1994) offers us a list of promotional materials that are also appropriate for faculty development initiatives. They include brochures, flyers, form letters, catalogues, posters, in-house newsletters, personal contacts, electronic mail, and electronic bulletin boards. These materials should clearly disclose full information about the programs, including the topic, faculty application, presenter format, and length of sessions. The more information that is distributed, the more faculty can assess whether and how the program will be helpful to them. This contributes to realistic expectations on the part of the faculty.

Additionally, materials that provide a clear picture of the need, objectives, and format of the sessions need to be prepared and distributed. These materials should stress the relevance of the sessions. Explicitly making connections for faculty to their context in this way will improve faculty participation. Distribution of this information also demonstrates a climate of respect for faculty. The publicity should also personalize the invitation to participate, so that it will not be perceived as an impersonal institutional bid for faculty development attendance. The tone of communications can influence faculty participation.

Another important component of promotion is to establish an effective channel for distributing information to prospective participants. We cannot make assumptions regarding how faculty want to be informed. This information needs to be obtained directly from the faculty through needs assessment, advisory groups, and environmental scanning. By identifying and using a channel consistently, faculty development initiatives will be expected on a regular basis. This lends structure and may reserve space in the busy faculty member's calendar for the programs.

In one case, faculty participation in a new series of faculty development programs was moderate one year and much lower the next. Conversations with participants revealed that all faculty members did not receive advance written announcement of the programs because the promotional packets were not distributed. In fact, in some departments, only those faculty who inquired of the faculty development office found out about the upcoming programs. A different information channel was used the next year which also proved ineffective—the material went to the department heads, but was never passed on to individual faculty in their mailboxes.

Issues of concern in promoting faculty development efforts also include the timing of publicity and of the session itself. Sufficient lead time and reminders to faculty need to be incorporated into this timeline. One of the certain ways to spoil a program is to give inadequate notice. Lead time offers the opportunity to plan, rearrange schedules, ask questions, and discuss the forthcoming events, rather than trying to add sessions to a harried schedule.

Developers should look for commitment from the faculty in attending the programs. Here registration affords many benefits. Since faculty have many demands competing for their time—teaching loads, research requirements, advising students, and service on committees, to name a few—we cannot assume that they are readily available for programs. Registration involves commitment on the part of faculty members and increases their likelihood of participation. It formalizes the faculty's anticipated attendance and reduces the chance of minor circumstances interrupting their plans. The participant list will have many uses for the developer and the presenter. Such a list serves to distribute pre-session and follow-up materials readily. The presenter, if from outside the institution, may also consult the developer to learn more about the needs of the anticipated participants prior to the session. This can help in appropriate and meaningful preparation of the learning experience.

Registration also aids in determining an accurate number of anticipated participants. This information is necessary to ensure that enough rooms of the right size are scheduled for the program. It also ensures that enough materials and refreshments, if included, are prepared. Adult learners value the materials they receive in learning experiences and feel disengaged and deprived when there are insufficient amounts of materials available. Refreshments always offer an opportunity to meet physical and social needs of participants involved in lengthy programs, but are a complication if they are insufficient or not easily accessible.

The degree to which organizational support is evident will often influence the success of faculty development. The opportunities available for the promotion of the program are a measure of the level of organizational support. Cervero and Wilson (1994) discuss the importance of understanding the organization and power hierarchies within an institution and their impact on programming. Where the program is tied to the organizational mission and endorsed by the leadership, greater visibility and endorsement will be evident. One way this may be accomplished is by having representatives from each department and the administration on a faculty advisory committee.

Finally, the developer may cast the faculty development initiative in the context of the campus as a whole and see if there is a way to view it as a positive event on campus. Being able to do so may offer opportunities to garner the support of other campus organizations or committees, giving the program greater visibility and importance.

> *When Judy Maskowitz, chair of the Women's Studies Department, was preparing to schedule a noted author on gender equity in the classroom for a workshop on campus, she realized that this presented an opportunity for all faculty on campus. After informing the chair of the college's Faculty Development Advisory Committee of the workshop, Women's Studies and the Advisory Committee collaboratively sponsored and promoted the event. This resulted in a larger audience for the event than originally anticipated. As an added benefit of this cooperative effort, faculty development was perceived as a positive event contributing to the sense of collegiality and goodwill among faculty and across organizational hierarchies within the institution.*

We turn next to the actual presentation and delivery of the program, which affords opportunities to incorporate all of our themes and principles regarding adult learning.

Implementing Adult Learning Principles

The goal of this book is to enhance the effectiveness of faculty development through thoughtful and systematic planning based on the theories of adult learning. Perhaps the most obvious application of this is in the Delivery Stage. It is here that the presenter has the opportunity to put into action a truly learner-centered experience. As strange as it may seem, it is our experience that well-meaning adult educators may forget about their knowledge of adult learners and, for example, present programs in a strictly nonparticipatory fashion. This task ensures that both developer and presenter focus on the application of adult learning principles in delivering the program to participants. Faculty developers should be looking for a presenter who will work with them to incorporate these principles into the presentation and who is not opposed to such a collaborative process.

A learner-centered program will address the needs of the faculty, utilize their knowledge and experience, and emphasize application to their professional duties. Participation in active learning strategies during a program is one way that these principles should be enacted. Such involvement may reference the expertise and experience of the faculty as well as encourage them to determine how to put what they are learning into action. Active learning strategies can guard against two frequent criticisms of faculty development: "It was boring," and "It is irrelevant to my work."

The developer works from the basis of what the faculty see as their learning needs. This should result in more cooperation and willingness to change as the program proceeds. Indeed, this learner-centeredness has been the emphasis of the proliferation of centers for teaching excellence and of instructional developers that have been designated by higher education institutions to assist the faculty in their individual and collective academic pursuits (Millis, 1994).

At this point, we suggest asking several questions about how the program's format and strategies emulate adult learning principles:

- How can the learners best participate?
- How can they use their experience in the learning process?
- How can session content be made relevant?

For example, although the institution may be advocating the use of technology in teaching, in some cases, the latest and greatest technological advances may not be the best methods for presentation (King, 1998a, 1998b). In one case, participants in a two-day in-residence workshop listened to presenters and then used an electronic forum to post their ideas and questions about the presentations. While some of the presenters responded to most of the queries, others did not at all. Participants were left with a reduced voice and less dynamic discussion than would have been afforded by using the available face-to-face format. The program had the added benefit of some participants using a new technical tool, but the content and level of buy-in for the program suffered. The important point here is that the methods and goals of the program need to be matched in order to gain the greatest benefit of active learning for the participants. Case studies provide opportunities to apply new concepts to real-life situations, while inquiry-based learning places the learner in an experiential mode for learning. Additionally, focused discussion groups, collaborative projects, action plans, and question and answer sessions are ways to explore the meaning of new learning (Brookfield, 1990).

Finally, the methods of learning and teaching should be in a form that the faculty desire and are comfortable with. For instance, oftentimes faculty want to learn about technology from a hands-on perspective (King, 1998b; Lawler & Wilhite, 1997) rather than just a presentation or discussion about it. If developers ignore this desire, then faculty will be discontented with the sessions and may not continue to participate in them. Very often it is active participation that faculty seek in faculty development initiatives. This focus on the learner's desire and active participation embodies adult learning principles and will promote successful development experiences (Gordon & Levinson, 1990; King, 1998b; Wilhite, DeCosmo & Lawler, 1996). Methods incorporating faculty experiences include using case studies devised ahead of time or concurrently, based on their experiences, and inquiring about their level of experience in order to gauge the presentation content and pace. A critical incident questionnaire is also useful in that it provides participants with specific and significant information (Brookfield, 1990, 1995). In using the critical incident questionnaire, the participant identifies a single incident from work and then critically reflects on and analyzes its meaning, consequences, and alternatives.

Efforts to tailor the programs to participant experience are well received by faculty. This may be done through building on the program's lesson by developing personal or group-action plans and through case studies, case stories, or strategic planning. Finally, the developer should continually seek ways to make the learning relevant to those experiences. This may be done by using problem solving or inquiry-based teaching methods. The more fully faculty members can see application to their situations, the more positive their experience with the program will be. Emphasizing the application of learning is a fundamental tenet of successful adult learning experiences.

Monitoring the Program

After the program begins, the faculty developer plays a leading role in the outcomes by monitoring, troubleshooting, and learning from the program. A program left unmonitored may fall prey to a multitude of problems that could have been prevented or corrected. The alert faculty developer has many evaluative functions during the sessions including circulating and visiting sessions in progress, determining the climate of the rooms and comfort of participants, keeping the program on schedule, monitoring traffic flow, and being an effective facilitator. The importance of these functions as an essential part of an effective program cannot be overstated; programs may succeed or fail on the basis of just one or two of these components.

As the program proceeds, the developer confronts several issues in seeking ways to facilitate the experience. The timing, participants, and presenters may all be seen as the foci of troubleshooting efforts. Many times multisession programs run into difficulty with scheduling as sessions go over their time limit. Adjustments to the printed or previously announced schedule need to be made carefully and announced clearly so all participants can follow the schedule smoothly. Changes should be made considering both the individual parts and the whole program. Changes should also be kept to a minimum because they can be sources of much confusion among participants.

The welfare of the participants should also be monitored

as the program continues. Room temperatures, weather conditions, and pace of sessions are a few of the variables that need to be checked. The presenters also require attention. Someone should be designated to deal with technical, equipment, and physical needs (such as water) for each individual session. Additionally, program facilitators for each session can better assure that the session format is followed, such as making time for discussion, a question and answer period, and session time limits. Such facilitators greatly contribute to the success of programs.

The developer also needs to have some contingency plans for unexpected complications. Certain problems may be anticipated and prepared for before the program begins. These include equipment failure, presenter absence, delayed starts, and insufficient attendance. The development of troubleshooting teams, creative alternatives, and backup equipment are among solutions that may be planned. Having a prepared plan of action to deal with both specific and general problems will reduce the stress of monitoring the program and increase the success of the efforts.

Other tasks of the developer while the program is in progress are those of gathering data for the next stage and summarizing the program experience. While a full reflective perspective of the program will be realized in the final stage of the process, it cannot be accomplished without gathering information at this point. Developers should be engaged in formative evaluation of the program while it is in progress to determine what they can learn from the experience. Very often this takes the form of assuming the perspective of someone else; in this case it will be the participants, the presenters, and the sponsoring administration, to name a few.

THE DELIVERY STAGE AT WORK

Our opening scenario at Lawking College could have been quite different had the tasks described in this chapter been followed. Consideration of the following Delivery Stage questions would have provided a better platform for the program:

- Are we continuing to build on our preparation?
- How do we effectively promote the program?
- How are adult learning principles implemented?
- How do we monitor the program?

For example, if Rhonda McWilliams, the faculty developer, had relied on her preparation from previous workshops, she would have built on their strengths and met the overall goals of the college and the program. This would have been beneficial because faculty would have been already prepared to consider the topic at hand, and successive programs could have continued to delve deeper into the content area. Instead, this faculty development program appears to have been a one-shot approach to a very large topic that left faculty members confused and dissatisfied.

Second, Rhonda could have worked with the presenter to ensure that adult learning principles were used as guides in the presentation. In this scenario, the presenter seemed to expect the faculty to be mere spectators, rather than active participants. Including opportunities to discuss the faculty's interest in, needs regarding, and experience with the topic would have modeled the climate of collaboration so important in adult learning. Another major adult learning principle, valuing the adult learners, needed to be considered. When the learners are valued, it will be evident in the attitude and accommodating actions of the presenter. When considerate action is taken to correct or prevent problems that participants face, it is evident that value is placed on people; and with this, a positive and cooperative climate can emerge.

Finally, Rhonda's monitoring and troubleshooting of the session could have prevented some of the problems with the format of the program by facilitating the session in accordance with the expected and desired format. This scenario demonstrates that it is appropriate and wise to ask presenters how they are intending to conduct their sessions. This is a good way for them to express an expectation and preference for a particular format. The consequence of not having such input with the presenter was a major stumbling block in the Lawking College workshop. The faculty expected and wanted a "hands-on" session, and when they did not receive it, many of them left.

Rhonda could have benefited from knowledge of the Adult Learning Model of Faculty Development's Delivery Stage. With the improvements suggested, her faculty development program would have been aligned for greater success.

SUMMARY

The Delivery Stage of the Adult Learning Model for Faculty Development has provided a broad framework from which to present specific faculty development initiatives. The major tasks of this stage are building on the preparation, promoting the program, implementing adult learning principles, and monitoring the program. This chapter has discussed the tasks, issues and concerns, strategies, and guidelines for conducting faculty development programs that will incorporate adult learning principles. The importance of tying programs to the organization, its mission, and the goals of faculty development on that campus, the use of effective communication channels with the faculty, and the need to integrate adult learning principles have been highlighted as particularly important to the Delivery Stage. In addition, this framework has offered a view of the program through the eyes of a specific group of adult learners, the faculty. Recognizing adult learner needs, presenting participatory and active learning programs, and emphasizing application have been specifically discussed.

CHAPTER 6

Follow-up

Every fall Central State University has held an orientation for its adjunct faculty. This event is always greeted with enthusiasm among the adjuncts since it makes them feel a part of the university community. The academic dean is responsible for organizing the one-night event each year. Two years ago, her colleague, Barbara Murray, director of adult studies, approached the dean with the idea of offering a workshop for the faculty on active learning. The dean agreed to include the workshop in the orientation events and provided funding for the presenter and other costs associated with the workshop. The following year Barbara again made a suggestion for a workshop to be included in the orientation, and the dean agreed to support another workshop.

This year Barbara again approached the dean with another topic for what she planned as the third annual faculty development workshop. However, with the university in a cost containment period, the dean was not as forthcoming as in past years. The dean asked Barbara for a report on the previous two workshops. This report was to include the following: how the participants had evaluated these learning events, how the workshop had made a difference in their teaching, and how Barbara had supported the changes faculty were presumably making in their classrooms. If the workshops had been effective and Barbara could provide information on this, then the dean would consider funding a third workshop for the coming fall. Barbara was in a dilemma. She knew from talking with her faculty that they enjoyed the workshops and found them helpful, but she had only anedoctal information. She had not done a systematic evaluation and follow-up and therefore had nothing concrete to substantiate the informal assessment of the program.

INTRODUCTION TO THE
FOLLOW-UP STAGE

Throughout the earlier chapters we have focused on how important it is to incorporate evaluation and reflection in the planning and offering of the faculty development programs. These processes continually provide valuable information for those working with faculty. The Follow-up Stage is the time to collect all that information, along with summative data, to create a total picture of the faculty development program. Barbara's story is one we often hear. Evaluation and follow-up are topics written about regularly but often neglected in practice. Even in cases where faculty development events are evaluated, researchers found that the data was rarely used in further planning (Chism & Szabo, 1997–1998). Formal, systematic assessment of faculty development projects may be rare, while anedoctal reports and workshop "smile sheets" may be the norm. If we had been working with Barbara from the beginning, we would have encouraged her to ask herself several questions and then consider three tasks, which would provide her with information and evidence to support her work. The questions for the Follow-up Stage are:

• What is our evaluation plan?
• How will ongoing support be provided for what was learned?
• What can we, as faculty developers, gain from reflecting on our role in this endeavor?

These questions guide the faculty developer through the final process. This assessment of both the event and the role of the faculty developer is becoming more and more important today with the increase in attention to outcomes assessment in higher education. Barbara's colleague and supervisor, the academic dean, requires evidence of the outcomes of Central State University's workshops. Such accountability goes beyond cost and time benefits and includes quality and improved performance (Brown & Seidner, 1998), making evaluation and follow-up critical issues in any program. If we expect to provide effective programs with specific outcomes as well as opportunities for change and growth, then we need to document and measure our accomplishments and create an environment conducive to continuing the learning started in the faculty development event.

In this chapter, we take a look at the Follow-up Stage. This will include the summative evaluation process for the faculty development program as well as the assessment of the role of a faculty developer. We are also interested in how the organizational environment can support the new learnings and what needs to be done to encourage faculty to implement information and skills learned in their daily practice.

ADULT LEARNING PRINCIPLES

In Chapter 2 we introduced the principles of adult learning that facilitate faculty development and provide a conceptual framework from which to make the Adult Learning Model for Faculty Development a reality. Each stage has relied on these principles to enhance the faculty development process. This fourth stage, Follow-up, is no exception. In fact, as we enter the final stage of our faculty development plan and initiative, we see how the principles are woven into the model and reinforce what we have done at each stage. The adult learning principles inherent in the Follow-up Stage center on the goal of empowering the participants in their professional roles. If we build in a climate of respect and provide opportunities for collaboration and participation, we enhance the possibility that learning will take place. Implementing what we have learned empowers faculty and helps them to make the changes necessary to continue in our complex world. Hence the importance at this stage of the principles of climate of respect, collaboration, learning for action, and empowering the participants.

Just as the faculty were engaged in the planning process, now it is time to engage them again in the evaluation and assessment of the program. Building on earlier efforts, this continual involvement demonstrates a **climate of respect,** as both participation and feedback are indicators of a respectful climate (Lawler, 1991). Faculty are traditionally schooled in research and critical analysis. Their skills may be very helpful in establishing evaluation plans. Here is another opportunity for **utilization of their experiences in a collaborative way.**

The goals and objectives of most faculty development programs are to motivate faculty to change by implementing their new learnings into their classrooms and institutional settings. This requires that "modified beliefs and assumptions get translated into actual behavioral change" (Licklider, Schnelker & Fulton, 1997–1998, p. 127). Opportunities should be afforded the faculty to come to an understanding of the new learning, take action on the learning, reflect on the process, and then use those reflections to apply insights to future situations (Brookfield, 1995; Lawler, 1991). **Learning for action** provides the faculty with not only theory, but also practical applications.

Finally, the adult learning literature urges us to build in opportunities for **empowerment** (Lawler, 1991). Empowerment is described as "the creative and dynamic possibilities of education as a means of change" (Gadotti, 1994, p. 81). As learners become aware of their situation through education and self-reflection, they may become empowered to make changes and take action (Merriam & Caffarella, 1999). While the model of empowerment education has been adopted in many adult education settings, such as literacy, it has yet to be incorporated into faculty development. Integrating the concept of empowerment here will guide the faculty to see how new learning can be used in their work, especially how it connects with their own teaching and learning. King (1998c, 1999) reports that gaining a sense of empowerment through a professional development activity can stimulate self-confidence. It can also promote an acceptance and tolerance for change, and encourage risk taking.

As the faculty development program comes to closure and the developer begins the assessment, it is important to keep these principles in mind. Just as we saw them as a foundation for needs assessment in the Preplanning Stage, they are applicable to tasks such as a formal evaluation. They are also applicable to the faculty developer's assessment. For just as the faculty are encouraged to learn and grow throughout this process, so too are faculty developers as they reflect on their roles. In doing so they become models for the participants. With these concepts in mind, each task and its related issues will be discussed for the Follow-up Stage.

FOLLOW-UP TASKS AND ISSUES

In planning for faculty development, much attention is paid to the creation and delivery of the programs. Traditionally, we have come to expect that program participants assume responsibility for implementing their learning in a successful way. Additionally, evaluation of programs has been limited to immediate feedback. For many faculty developers, the process ends with the end of the program. We would like to expand this perspective and encourage faculty developers to see this Follow-up Stage as an opportunity to continue the learning, which began in the program. It is also an opportunity to gain information and support for future successful programming. As we saw with Barbara at Central State University, her planning had left her without the kind of information she needed to continue her plans for working with the faculty. We suggest that Barbara take a different perspective by asking the questions and utilizing the tasks of this Follow-up Stage of the Adult Learning Model for Faculty Development. These tasks go beyond standard evaluation techniques and emphasize transfer of learning and effective change while creating systematic documentation of the entire faculty development initiative.

Follow-up encompasses more than evaluating the program. It is also concerned with a self-assessment of the role of the faculty developer. This creates an opportunity for learning for the person responsible for the program and its implementation. This holistic approach will prepare Barbara to not only answer her dean's requests, but substantiate both her role as an effective faculty developer and the faculty's success in learning. The three Follow-up Stage tasks are:

- Evaluating
- Continuing the learning
- Assessing the faculty developer's role

We will consider each of these tasks, the steps involved in accomplishing each one, and the issues and concerns we encounter.

Evaluating

Similar to the concept of needs assessment, program evaluation has a vast literature to aid faculty developers in assessing programs. First and foremost in this literature is the consensus that evaluation is necessary and useful. As we have seen in earlier chapters, evaluation is an ongoing process to facilitate the success of the program. Here we will look at summative evaluation, the method for measuring to what extent the educational event achieved its goals after the program is completed (Parrott, 1998), and its importance for program assessment and future planning. Kirkpatrick (1998) cites three reasons for such evaluation. First he sees evaluation providing concrete justification for the programming and the personnel responsible for the program. Continuing the learning and future planning of programs are his second reason for undertaking evaluation. Finally, he reminds us of the most common reason for evaluation, that is, "to determine the effectiveness of a program and ways in which it can be improved" (p. 97). Since faculty development programs may be tenuous on campus, as with Barbara's efforts at Central

State University, evaluation results may be necessary for the continuance of programming.

Evaluation results have another benefit in the arena of faculty development. As faculty provide information on the success of programming, they become important allies for encouraging their colleagues to engage in future efforts. In constructing a systematic evaluation plan, it is important to keep these three reasons in mind, along with institutionally specific reasons the developer may also have. Understanding the why of evaluation is critical for developing a useful plan (Chen, 1990). This plan should consist of the design of the evaluation including how it fits into the overall goals of the program and builds on the formative evaluation that has been occurring throughout the process.

There are several methods of evaluation that can be used at the end of the program. The faculty developer will need to decide which method is congruent with the philosophy of the educational event and which is practical and realistic to implement. Such methods include questionnaires, interviews, tests, performance reviews, case studies, and organizational records and documents (Caffarella, 1994; Parrott, 1998). We would also like to add that in higher education, student class evaluations, peer review, and self-assessment by the faculty may also be used to collect data regarding changes that occurred as a result of the professional development activity. Collaboration with both the faculty participants in the event and the administrators who have a stake in professional development is crucial in selecting the appropriate summative evaluation methods. We encourage faculty developers to use more than one method if at all possible. This provides a more complex and thorough description of what took place within the program and what outcomes were achieved. Remember, the purpose of evaluation is not only to measure how well the program met its objectives, but also to provide some description of the learning which took place, as well as any changes which occur as a result of the event.

In selecting the appropriate methods to assess outcomes, it is necessary to understand the organizational cultural and politics that impact evaluation. Who will use the data and to what ends? Cervero and Wilson (1994, 1996) urge us to consider this social context in all aspects of planning, and we see this especially important in the Follow-up Stage. Evaluation will provide us with information upon which we can make practical judgments regarding programming and the purposes it serves. For example, sensitive collected data may need to be confidential and power relationships may need to be understood to avoid misuses of the data. In some instances, evaluation is seen as a threat for this reason. It is important to understand the perceptions of faculty with regard to the evaluation process. Finally, the evaluator's role needs to be reviewed for bias within the organizational context.

We are most familiar with evaluation data that is collected immediately at the end of a seminar, workshop, or class. Simple forms asking questions about how participants liked the program are often used. These forms measure satisfaction with everything from the room setup to the instructor's presentation skills and provide an immediate overview of participants' feelings. However, they tell us little about the actual learning that may have occurred and the changes faculty may make as a result of the event. Therefore, it is helpful and productive to use another evaluation method some time after the event. The reasons for the evaluation, such as Barbara's report, can drive the selection of the method. Barbara may choose to interview selected faculty members at the end of the semester to find out whether or not they have implemented active learning in their classrooms. During her interviews, Barbara could ask about not only the implementation of active learning techniques, but also the reactions of students to the new instructional methods and the faculty's assessment of them. The goal is to see, after a period of time, what was really useful from the workshop.

The next step is analyzing the data. As noted earlier, many evaluations occur in training venues, but little is done with the data. We urge the faculty developer to see evaluation data as an integral part of the program. Caffarella (1994) tells us to be clear about our data analysis procedures. Before we collect the data, we need to understand exactly what questions we are trying to answer and where the data will be reported. We need to also consider the resources, financial and human, that will be needed for the process (Kowalski, 1988). Here too is a place to invite faculty collaboration, utilizing expertise in research and analysis from individual faculty members who have experience in evaluation and teach courses in research. Their expertise can include designing the evaluation tools, analyzing the data and preparing reports. Formalized reports are useful in gathering support for the program and providing the faculty developer with information for continuous needs assessment and program planning.

In reflecting on evaluation, the faculty developer may be challenged with several issues. As mentioned above, these evaluations take place within the social context of the organization. "The nature of evaluation itself raises ethical questions because it involves judgment: Decisions have to be made as to who and what are judged" (Merriam & Caffarella, 1992, p. 295). Values, biases, and experiences of all those involved in the evaluation process influence these decisions. Conflicts and ethical dilemmas may arise to challenge the faculty developer. Developing an ethical sensitivity, that is, an awareness that judgments and decisions may have an ethical dimension, can be advantageous (Lawler, 1998). Asking questions about fairness, potential harm, and the violation of laws, professional codes, and organizational policies are useful in gaining this awareness (Zinn, 1998).

Another evaluation issue centers on resources. The faculty developer must be aware of the time evaluation takes, the financial requirements, and the staffing available to create, conduct, and analyze. Selection of methods for collecting the data may be limited due to budget constraints. Professional responsibilities may preclude the faculty developer from conducting follow-up interviews or focus groups. Lack of technology may prohibit statistical analysis of collected data. Being aware of resources is imperative in planning the procedures for evaluation.

Evaluation is a powerful, sometimes threatening, process. It provides information, offers occasions for learning, and creates opportunities to build alliances within the organization. Reflecting on both the formative and summative evaluation of the program can lead the faculty developer to the next task in the Follow-up Stage—continuing the learning.

Continuing the Learning

Most program planning books end with the evaluation process. However, any professional development activity will continue to affect various constituencies within the organization. Building on the concepts of support and transfer of learning introduced in Chapter 4, we recommend that the faculty development process continue through a series of important and helpful functions. Returning to Central State University and Barbara's dilemma, it is apparent that she considered each faculty development workshop as a unique event. Armed with positive responses, Barbara was comfortable with proposing a new workshop each year. Within the climate of fiscal restraint and program accountability, however, her dean saw the need for concrete information and data supporting successful outcome goals and change. Continuing to assess the program's outcomes and considering what transfer of learning took place would have been beneficial for Barbara.

Caffarella (1994) defines the transfer of learning as "the effective application by program participants of what they learned" (p. 108). It needs to be considered right from the start of program planning. The Follow-up Stage is the time to see if it has occurred. Are the faculty applying what they have learned in their daily work? One method is to incorporate various questions and measurements in the evaluation process that focus on the changes planned for in the educational event. "Without clear and doable plans for how participants can apply what they have learned, it is often difficult to trace how program activities are related to program outcomes and to provide justification for judgments made on the worth and value of a program" (Caffarella, 1994, p. 116). Here is where we need to develop specific questions to answer and indicators to observe in collecting data on transfer of learning. For example, following the workshop in active learning which demonstrated several instructional methods, Barbara could ask the faculty who attended if they are using any of the methods in their classroom. She could continue the inquiry with questions related to the faculty's perception of the success of these methods and their comfort with using them. Also, it would be important to find out whether or not the faculty would continue to use the new techniques and whether faculty felt that the techniques had a positive effect in the classroom.

Assessing transfer of learning, along with evaluating the program for participant satisfaction and objective criteria, can be interpreted as part of continual needs assessment. As more and more colleges and universities plan professional development for their faculty, it is important to incorporate this type of assessment into the overall mission and goals of the institution. As the goal of enhancing teaching and learning takes shape and drives faculty development initiatives, the program development moves beyond the one-shot approach. If we are engaged in ongoing faculty development, programs presented on a regular basis from year to year, then ongoing assessment is crucial for the effectiveness of these endeavors. This process should include, among other things, a consideration of the impact of all professional development on the organization and its faculty. The faculty developer is in a unique position to lead the institution in change by providing crucial data related to these professional development events and their long-term outcomes for faculty, students, and the college.

Another aspect of this task is support. Without support on several levels, transfer of learning, positive outcomes, and new programming are unlikely (King, 1998c; King & Lawler, 1998). Change does not occur in a vacuum. Faculty will need support to make changes in their professional work as a result of the new learning. As we have seen earlier, faculty who feel supported in making changes and innovations in their work will seek out professional development opportunities. If this support continues after the event, it is likely that implementation and transfer of learning will occur. This calls for an organizational context in which the people, structure, and cultural milieu of the institution value continuous learning and development (Caffarella,

1994). As a faculty developer it is important to assess this organizational context and identify support systems for the faculty participants. A good example of this comes from a midsize university, which recently offered several hands-on workshops on creating multimedia presentations for classroom use. The faculty developer made sure that Instructional Media Services was available and willing to work individually with faculty after the workshop to customize their presentations and continue learning the steps involved. In fact, the director of the department extended invitations on many occasions and through many institutional delivery systems to faculty to come to the department to work on their projects with guided help. The support of continuous learning and help with implementation of new skills was provided. However, what the faculty developer did not foresee was the growth in interest in using multimedia techniques, not only by those who attended the workshops, but among faculty who were learning these teaching tools on their own. At the end of the semester it was announced at the faculty meeting that the demand for classrooms that could support multimedia presentations had outgrown the number of classrooms available. So popular was this new teaching tool that many faculty who requested equipped classrooms were unable to get them for the spring semester. The faculty felt frustrated having first been encouraged to learn new skills, only to come to a dead end because of planning issues and lack of resources. Full support was not in place to complement the faculty development initiative.

As we have seen in Chapter 4, when the faculty developer identifies topics for professional development, it is important at that point to consider the support available for continuous learning and its implementation in the work of the faculty. Our example highlights two areas of support. First, positive support was available from the personnel in Instructional Media Services. They were ready to assist faculty with their new learning and eager to help them apply it to specific course material. Second, the technology resources to support the faculty in their new learning were lacking. As more and more faculty become skilled in technology, campuses must prepare to meet this need. This requires long-range planning, significant financial resources, and a commitment from the administration (King, 1998b). The faculty developer may have little or no direct influence over these significant factors. What the faculty developer does have control over is the planning and implementation of the program. With faculty asking for new learnings in technology as in the above example, the faculty developer must assess the situation for support after the professional development program occurs. Our developer did arrange for Instruction Media Services to support the new learning. Next our developer could have assessed the classroom situation and done two things: one, talk with faculty during the program about the demands for classrooms and encourage them to put their requests in early; and two, communicate to the administration regarding the potential demand and its long-range implications. These two areas of support, help with implementation and available resources, are important for faculty to feel comfortable with their new skills and for the success of transfer of learning (King, 1998a, 1998b).

Another area of support that is critical to consider concerns faculty assessment and rewards. As we have seen in Chapter 1, professional development needs to be tied into faculty reward systems. The faculty developer must be aware of these systems, including the requirements for promotion, tenure, and merit raises. These systems may vary from department to department within an institution; however, it is essential that the faculty developer gain an understanding of the requirements and standards surrounding the faculty's responsibility in their discipline and in their department. It is important that the goals of professional development be aligned with the reward system and that the faculty see this connection. In a university that places great emphasis on research and funding, where promotions and salary increases are tied to the amount of grants a faculty brings into the institution and the number of publications reporting research results one has, there may be little incentive to improve classroom teaching. However, in a college where teaching is critical for promotion, support may be available on all levels to enhance the effectiveness of what happens in the classroom. Here faculty development initiatives around instructional methods, such as active learning and transformative teaching, would be welcomed (King, 1997, 1998c; King & Lawler, 1998). An important area to consider is how faculty are evaluated in their classrooms. Will these evaluations take into consideration new changes? Will faculty feel comfortable making changes without risking negative assessments? If faculty developers have an understanding of the various reward systems, how the faculty will be supported through changes, and the administration's stance regarding change, they have a clearer idea of what support faculty will have to implement their new learning.

There is a way in which the faculty developer can be influential in creating support for the faculty after the program is completed. It takes advantage of the concept of collegiality by establishing network teams and mentoring opportunities within departments and across the institution. Although faculty are considered independent mavericks, many have experience working in teams, mentoring students, and participating in the shared governance of the institution. Building on these experiences, the faculty developer can initiate collaborative opportunities for support following a professional development program. For example, when offering a series of seminars on cooperative learning for the college classroom, the developer may first identify faculty who are already successfully using this instructional method in their classrooms. The next step would be to invite these faculty to participate in the seminars by sharing their experiences, bringing actual examples and stories that would illustrate their implementation strategies and their continuous learning. These faculty would then be asked to act as resources in a network following the seminar. This networking can be created on e-mail, occur at brown bag lunches, or take place with individuals in one-to-one consultations. Not only can faculty share the instructional changes and techniques learned in the seminar, but more important, they can explore the contextual issues which change brings. Setting up networks after the development initiative, creating resource lists, and establishing a core of consultants provide support to faculty and encourage active participation.

A successful faculty development initiative should go beyond the program itself. It involves "the design of work, work environments, technology, rewards, systems, structures and policies" (Watkins & Marsick, 1993, p. 44). It should also encompass what happens to the faculty as they implement their new learning. If the faculty find support for their new learning, they are likely to continue to learn, encourage other faculty to attend programs, and feel satisfied in their endeavors. But if support is lacking, faculty may feel frustrated, betrayed, and angry with not only the faculty developer but also the institution. Sharing these negative perceptions and attitudes with other faculty can produce obstacles for the faculty developer's future planning. Paulsen and Feldman (1995) warn us that faculty development for improved teaching requires "more than good will . . . More needs to be known about the existence and nature of various road blocks and how to remove them or get around them" (p. 132). They urge us to consider that "competing cultures, scarce resources, different sets of values about what is important, power differentials, intractable groups and people at today's colleges and universities all affect the implementation and effectiveness of programs" (p. 132). With this in mind, developers have an ethical obligation to plan responsibly (Cevero & Wilson, 1994; Lawler, 1998; Merriam & Caffarella, 1999). This means taking into consideration the organizational and political context and negotiating the interests of all involved in the outcomes of their development initiative. Such reflective exercises bring us back to considering the reflective practitioner, mentioned in Chapter 3, and the next task in the Follow-up Stage.

Assessing the Faculty Developer's Role

The final question to be asked during this Follow-up Stage centers on faculty developers and their role in the entire professional development process. This is the time to summarize the faculty development initiative from a holistic and retrospective position. This summary should include the learning outcomes and changes that have and are occurring within the individual faculty and the institution. It should also include an appraisal of the developer. We review not only what has changed as a result of the initiative, but also how effective we were. This assessment should include all evaluation reports, including follow-up interviews or surveys with participants, along with an environmental scan similar to the one described in Chapter 3. The faculty developer should also perform a self-assessment: "The ultimate foundation of all reflective practice or self-reflection is the ability and opportunity to engage in self-evaluation or self-assessment" (Paulsen & Feldman, 1995, p. 46). Using a self-assessment tool, such as the one presented in Appendix B or rereading a learning autobiography, described below, are practical ways to review the entire process and the effectiveness of the planning and delivery.

Many adult educators (Brockett, 1991; Brookfield, 1995; Cranton, 1996; Peters, 1991) have recommended a reflective period. Here it is important to consider what went right with the professional development initiative and what went wrong. Consideration should also be given to what could have been added and what needed to be changed. Goals, objectives, and potential outcomes should be reviewed and matched with what is now happening in the institution and among the faculty. This entire process can be reviewed using the developer's professional skills and expertise. It is an opportunity for learning and gaining insight into what makes effective planning.

Brookfield (1995) discusses the characteristics of desirable faculty developers. These include credibility, authenticity, respect, consistency, and responsiveness, along with practical experience and an understanding of the dilemmas and issues the faculty face in their everyday work. Brookfield encourages those working with adult learners to reflect on their work by using learning autobiographies, which involves keeping a log or journal of experiences and lessons learned. Upon completion of the faculty development initiative, it is imperative to take the time to analyze this learning autobiography for insights and meaning in conjunction with the effectiveness of the program and the measurement of the outcomes.

Program evaluations provide information regarding details of the program, and learning autobiographies provide a record of personal experiences. What is missing from this self-assessment are the perceptions and assessments of those throughout the institution who have been observing the event and the developer's role. Here is the opportunity to gain further insight into not only the specific program itself as it occurred in time and place within the organization, but also the overall picture of the developer's role within the organizational context. How do the faculty and the administration perceive the role of the developer? How did the developer negotiate power and interests throughout the process? In what way has the developer assumed a leadership role within the organization? Is the developer seen as an expert in the area of facilitating learning experiences for faculty? These are crucial questions and the developer should seek answers from the various constituencies throughout the university. The advisory committee, which has been a guide throughout the process, may now be called upon to assess the developer's role. It will be crucial to provide the committee with a framework for this assessment, one in which the information solicited will be helpful in planning future programs and eliciting support throughout the organization. It may also be helpful to identify two or three individuals from the various constituencies—faculty, administration, students— who will agree to be observers and meet with the developer for assessment. Their perspectives will complete the assessment picture.

THE FOLLOW-UP STAGE AT WORK

Barbara has a very practical reason to adapt the Follow-up Stage to her work in faculty development at Central State University. If her goal is to continue offering workshops at the beginning of each academic year which require her academic dean's support and financial resources, then Barbara needs to include in her planning an evaluative process for accountability. She needs to go beyond her anedoctal information to substantiate formal procedures and gather data to profile her work and the work of the faculty that have attended over the years. Barbara neglected to see the bigger picture, which includes the organizational climate and the importance of financial resources in creating and delivering programs. In an academic setting where accountability is in the limelight and motivating faculty to change is the challenge, Barbara now has the perfect opportunity to provide her dean and others with important information. This information may enhance her role, bringing attention to the good work she has done, and it may also provide a more realistic picture of the faculty and their enthusiasm for change and learning. These positive outcomes may be missed if the Follow-up Stage is not completed.

Asking the three Follow-up Stage questions, Barbara would begin a process that could provide her with the documentation her dean requires.

- What is our evaluation plan?
- How will ongoing support be provided for what was learned?
- What can we, as faculty developers, gain from reflecting on our role in this endeavor?

First, Barbara can create an evaluation plan that includes not only the anedoctal information she has been collecting, but also the systematic documentation of what the faculty saw as positive and negative about the experience. This plan would also include a follow-up survey among faculty to assess their use of active learning in their classrooms and their experiences with the skills learned in the workshops. By utilizing feedback from her advisory group, Barbara can begin an environmental scan to understand what is happening to the students and their learning as a result of the faculty's implementation of new instructional methodology. Collecting data from various sources including faculty, advisory committee, administrators, and students will provide Barbara with an overall picture of the impact of the workshops she has organized and delivered over the past two years. She can then present this to her dean along with a systematic plan for future workshops.

Beyond this assessment, Barbara needs to review her role as faculty developer. Here she can review her own learning and consider the value of the workshops to her role and responsibilities at Central State University. Taking time for this reflection can be seen as a professional development activity for Barbara herself. She is certainly aware that her dean has been supportive and is interested in continuing that support. Now it is Barbara's opportunity to provide a rationale and concrete data to continue that support.

SUMMARY

The Follow-up Stage of the Adult Learning Model for Faculty Development offers a systematic way to evaluate the professional development initiative and the developer's role. Assessment includes reviewing formative evaluation information and summative evaluation from the program itself, along with a period of reflection and environmental scanning. This process seeks to answer the three important questions posed during this stage. The three tasks included in this stage—evaluation, continuing the learning, and assessing the faculty developer's role— have been described in detail. All three tasks are grounded in adult learning theory and utilize critical aspects of adult education program planning. Each of these tasks relates to critical issues faculty developers face at the end of the program. Since the literature offers little on how to continue the learning and self-assessment, this chapter has discussed several strategies. Chapter 7 will consider the challenges facing the developer today, along with an invitation to put the Adult Learning Model for Faculty Development into action and lead effective faculty development programs.

CHAPTER 7

Effective Faculty Development in Action

Planning programs effectively, whether for faculty or other adult learners, takes more than a systematic and comprehensive model. The Adult Learning Model for Faculty Development provides even more than standard program development models by viewing the faculty as adult learners and providing a series of practical tasks based on the principles of adult education. Even with this model in hand, however, delivering educational programs over a period of time requires other conditions and factors which can be identified and nurtured as we maintain our effectiveness as successful faculty developers.

This chapter will explore faculty development from the perspective of the developers. Now that we have an efficient and workable model in place, several questions remain. For instance, how do we maintain its effectiveness with the faculty and the institution over time? What are the critical issues and challenges that we may continually face as we create learning opportunities for faculty in our institutions? As we look at each of these questions, we also must remember and reflect on our role as a faculty developer. How will we continue our own development to ensure our role is effective and rewarding? What will sustain us and what professional development strategies will increase our effectiveness? These questions face each of us as we tackle the work of educational planning. As we take this personal perspective we will raise those frequently asked questions all of us have and review how the Adult Learning Model for Faculty Development can help us to answer them.

MAINTAINING EFFECTIVE
FACULTY DEVELOPMENT

What are the critical issues and challenges that we continually face as we create learning opportunities for faculty in our institutions? How does the faculty developer maintain effectiveness in the midst of planning, implementing, and evaluating faculty development initiatives? While the Adult Learning Model for Faculty Development provides guidance, more is needed in order to sustain the efforts of such programs. We turn our attention to the critical issues and challenges that surface as faculty developers bring their programs to life on campus.

Critical Issues

Faculty developers face four critical issues as they work to offer faculty development programs in higher education:

1. Power issues

2. Resource issues

3. Support and transfer of learning issues

4. Ethical issues

Power Issues

As the fall semester got under way, the director of faculty development at Homer College, Ellen Lisk, contemplated the fact that a new vice president of academic affairs would be searched for and selected during this semester. In the past, the administration had not been especially interested in faculty development and Ellen realized that this change in leadership provided the opportunity she needed to strengthen that program on campus. Realizing that an effective faculty development program depends on the acceptance and support of several key constituencies, Ellen decided to pay a visit to the dean of the School of Education to enlist the assistance of the school's faculty in campuswide faculty development. Ellen broached the purpose of her visit saying, "With the forthcoming changes in administration, I believe the time is right to reconfirm our commitment to faculty development for the entire college. I would like to see your educational experts lead the way as we plan our new initiatives."

Knowing that changes in key college personnel bring opportunities for changes in programs, Ellen acted proactively to build bridges with a campus constituency. Actions on college campuses have both visible and hidden political agendas. To further the power and impact of the Faculty Development Office on campus, she had scanned the environmental climate and determined that enlisting the cooperation of the School of Education would serve several purposes. Such an alliance could support commitment of resources and personnel, promote visibility of faculty development efforts, and provide curricular direction from educational experts.

Much of what individuals try to accomplish in a higher education institution needs to take into account the players and their political agendas (Cervero & Wilson, 1994). Everyone is placed in a particular position to fill specific needs and it is in that individual's best interests to meet those needs. Often what happens within the administration and programs on campus is cooperation in order to advance the purposes and agendas of the people involved; this is how the organization moves forward. The effective faculty developer will plan and conduct programs in such a way that makes the best of this political system of trades and balance. Looking for opportune times to promote faculty development initiatives is one good strategy. Scanning the political horizon and charting a course that enlists the mutual cooperation of offices, programs, and schools are other ways to make the most of the situation.

Resource Issues

As faculty developers plan and conduct an ongoing program, the necessity of obtaining adequate resources becomes a stark reality. A financial commitment from the institution needs to be in place to sustain faculty development efforts. These include budgetary concerns, planning time, personnel training, administration, facilities, instructional materials and equipment, printing and publicity, and other program costs. In institutions where faculty development programs are new, this support may be accounted for in individual budgets, but to support ongoing efforts a separate budget just for faculty development purposes needs to be established. Careful budgetary planning will include projection of complete program costs so that resources, and consequently programs, are not caught short. *Administering Successful Programs for Adults* (Galbraith, Sisco & Guglielmino, 1997) provides useful assistance in budgetary planning.

Additionally, faculty development may be supported through special grants, awards, and subsidies to start programs and to explore innovative initiatives. Resources on campus, for example, the Development Office and the Office of Institutional Research, may be able to identify funding sources such as corporations, federal and foundation grants, and in-house grants. Individually, faculty developers can make use of the extensive sources on the Internet which provide information on grants and awards for faculty development initiatives. Programs that are grounded in solid program planning and educational theory, such as the Adult Learning Model for Faculty Development, and that extend development through research will be good candidates for such awards. Such financial support should be regarded as seed money to start new programs or initiatives, and the institution should be looked to for ongoing support beyond the initial stages of development.

Resources for faculty development extend beyond strictly financial concerns. In addition, the educational institution needs to readily provide facilities, equipment, and personnel. Many faculty development programs are dreamed of, but never become a reality because of a lack of resources. At a time when institutions are trying to use their resources at full capacity in order to balance budgets, commitment to faculty development will need to be demonstrated before allocation of such resources to this indirect revenue-producing function. The faculty developer must establish a solid case of the institutional benefits for supporting faculty development. Benefits related to institutional financial prosperity include greater faculty research and teaching productivity, increased student satisfaction with faculty teaching which in turn can lead to improved student retention, and greater institutional recognition because of faculty teaching, service, research, and publication. This recognition can bring acclaim to the institution in the academic community and benefit the admissions office in its recruitment and marketing strategies. When faculty development is presented to the administration in these terms, and supporting research and documentation are offered, resources for programs will be more available.

Support and Transfer of Learning Issues

In many ways, the success of faculty development programs rests in the hands of the faculty as they choose whether to use what has been presented to them. The effective faculty developer will plan and implement programs with this in mind. Such considerations can be met by including faculty representatives in all the program stages, but a critical element is what will happen after the program is over. This is determined by both the faculty and institution, as the following all too familiar scenario illustrates.

Woodbine College faculty were thrilled to be able to use the new computer lab for their workshop in XYZ, the latest statistical software. The college had been able to retain the services of professional trainer who was a motivational, knowledgeable, and proficient presenter on the software package and its application to academic research. Especially for this program, the computer lab had been loaded and configured so that each participant could use a limited version of XYZ during the session. Two weeks after the highly acclaimed program had finished, follow-up evaluations were distributed. The responses were startling. The faculty's attitudes had turned sour because they realized that the full XYZ software package had not been purchased by the college and was therefore unavailable for fac-

ulty use. The evaluations presented an impending disaster for faculty development programs as many of the faculty stated that the session had merely waved unattainable temptations in their faces. They said they would not participate in future programs because this one had wasted time and raised false hopes.

If faculty leave programs equipped and motivated to bring positive change to their work, they can only progress as far as the available resources will take them. As in the example above, if they learn to use the latest computer statistical software for their research, they obviously can only use it if it is readily available. Programs that introduce unavailable new tools and methods are tantalizing at best, and more often frustrating and demoralizing. Transfer of learning—using and putting into action new knowledge in context—is the essence of effective faculty development.

How can faculty developers increase transfer of learning? We must plan for it from the beginning and enlist the solid support of the institution. The stage is set with available resources, support, and problem solving. It is one thing to do this on paper in a tidy sequential plan, and another to accomplish it within an organization of policies, procedures, and personalities. But if transfer of learning is not accomplished, future programs may be in jeopardy as it will become increasingly difficult to enlist faculty attendance and cooperation. Being aware of the importance of the transfer of learning and mapping out the resources to facilitate it will be a substantial foundation for effective faculty development.

Ethical Issues

As with any endeavor involving people, questions about fairness and ethical obligations to our colleagues, the faculty, the institutional administration, and other stakeholders are sure to arise as we plan and deliver faculty development programming. Effective faculty developers will use an ethical perspective and thoughtful decision making to view the conflicts and dilemmas which arise as they negotiate interests. Therefore, it is imperative that we have a clear understanding of the ethical problems and issues we may face in our work.

Ethical problems arise when we are faced with a conflict of values. Values can be personal, professional, cultural, and institutional. The astute faculty developer will understand their various constituencies and how their values may conflict and create dilemmas. Identifying these conflicts as ethical dilemmas provides the faculty developer with a positive strategy to address the conflict and reach a solution. Zinn (1993) gives us useful questions to ask ourselves when we think we are being challenged with an ethical dilemma. She prompts us to focus first on the use of the words that we are using to describe the situation, such as "right" or "wrong" or "fair." She suggests we review any published codes and guidelines to see whether there may be a violation. Does this situation incur potential harm? Does it involve a conflict of values? Would we feel comfortable taking the same action in a "clean, well-lit room"? Her questions conclude with "Do I have a gut feeling that something is not quite 'right' about this?" (p. 8). These questions and tasks help us to recognize first that a situation has an ethical dimension and second that we have discomfort regarding it. From here we can begin to use ethical decision making.

> *John Reston felt conflicted about his new role as faculty developer for Tri-County Community College. Having just completed a needs assessment with the 58 faculty at this small rural institution, he was ready to make his recommendations for programming to the administration. Then John heard through the grapevine that the college was only interested in getting the poor teachers to attend in order to change their teaching techniques and that no matter what plan was presented, this would be the goal of the programming. He realized that while the faculty were led to believe that they had some input into the process, they had no real power to shape the agenda.*

Here we see misuse of faculty input and deception related to the goals of the program. John's conflict revolves around the issue of bogus empowerment which occurs when stakeholders are encouraged to think that they have been empowered, when in fact they have not (Ciulla, 1998). John's next step, now that he has identified his discomfort and recognized the situation as an ethical dilemma, is to decide what he should do about the situation.

The literature in adult education is very helpful in providing resources for models of ethical decision making (Fielder as cited in Lawler, 1998; Hiemstra, 1988; Lawler & Fielder, 1991; Walker, 1993; Zinn, 1993). Most of these models propose that we use a problem-solving framework in which we look at the ethical question, identify alternatives, and review ethical rules and principles, which can guide our choice of alternatives. We should also include in this process a consideration of the personal and organizational goals which may be at stake. Then with overall consideration for ethical obligations, goals, and practical matters, we select the best alternative. "Ethical decision making is ultimately a matter of striking a balance among conflicting demands" (Fielder, as cited in Lawler, 1998, p. 244).

For John Reston, decision making will include looking at all the stakeholders involved in the faculty development program and their values and concerns. If the administration is invested in improving poor teaching, John may want to share with the faculty that ultimately the goal of all faculty development is teaching effectiveness. He now may see alternatives to his dilemma in which he can balance the interests of all stakeholders in providing an honest and productive program plan. He may also try to persuade the administration that genuine faculty empowerment is essential to the success of faculty development.

Ethical dilemmas need not be unsolvable. Professional codes of ethics, guidelines for good practice, and the many writings of educators who are concerned with practical applications for everyday practice are available to aid us in our work.

Continuous Effectiveness

Maintaining effective faculty development necessitates a commitment. Even great faculty development programs cannot be left to continue unattended. Building upon the Adult Learning Model for Faculty Development, faculty development initiatives may be viewed from the perspective of six actions that will support such continued effectiveness:

1. Maintaining a holistic perspective

2. Applying adult learning principles

3. Involving faculty in every phase

4. Evaluating continually

5. Keeping the model flexible

6. Using the Faculty Development Checklist (Appendix A)

Maintaining a Holistic Perspective

As faculty developers keep in mind the entire Adult Learning Model for Faculty Development they are assisted in achieving effectiveness by maintaining a holistic perspective. This holistic perspective will serve to unify the model's individual stages. Sometimes when one focuses on individual, discreet steps as ends in themselves, the greater purposes of effective programs are lost. For example, the continuity of a goal and theme will cast ongoing faculty development programs into the "big picture" and not fracture the program with a multitude of dissociated efforts. When faculty development initiatives complement rather than compete with the mission and goals of the institution, the positive, enduring effect of such programs is increased. There will be a progressively magnified effect as the programs build on and complement one another.

Applying Adult Learning Principles

Additionally, effective faculty development needs to diligently and consistently incorporate adult learning principles. Opportunities to infuse the planning process with a learner-centered, in this case faculty-centered, focus should not be lost. This will communicate a clear message of respect to the faculty. When faculty are esteemed as valued adult learners, their cooperation will be greater, the programs will be more appropriate to their needs and wants, and they will be learning the value of employing the principles through their experience. While teaching adult learning principles may not be the chief, direct outcome of a session, it can be an important indirect outcome of effective faculty development.

Involving Faculty in Every Phase

Faculty development programs that are imposed by the administration, or its representatives, upon the faculty are not well received (Candy, 1996). Instead, faculty involvement has many benefits for the faculty and the program, ultimately increasing the effectiveness of the program. This faculty involvement can take many forms such as forming a faculty advisory committee and utilizing faculty expertise. This format promotes the important outcomes we strive for—consensus in decisions, program direction, and participant support.

Faculty involvement can prevent many of the real and perceived objections or problems that can arise from administrative control. Truly authentic involvement by the faculty will ensure that bogus empowerment, mentioned earlier, is avoided. In addition, faculty, by their very profession, often possess expertise and contacts in areas that may be needed for programs. As they are consulted as resources, and possibly presenters, the ownership of the program moves more into their hands. In addition, their input will be valuable in crafting a program that is relevant and valuable to their colleagues. Anticipation, cooperation, and participation can enhance the effectiveness of the programs.

Evaluating Continually

For programs to be effective, evaluation needs to be interwoven throughout the planning. Such evaluation shifts focus throughout the different stages of the Adult Learning Model for Faculty Development, emphasizing the organization, resources, needs of the faculty, progress of the program, or outcomes. For example, interpreting needs assessment results entails evaluation of current needs and whether they align with either expectations or organizational goals. This evaluative process includes looking at the current information and trying to find a fit that will match with stakeholders' needs and interests.

Additionally, formative evaluation is evident as developers serve variously as facilitators, monitors, and troubleshooters. By engaging in these functions, problems are not left to be dealt with after the fact. Instead, they are recognized, confronted, and, we hope, solved while the program is in progress. This allows the program to be a success despite the many things that can (and will) go wrong. Similarly, retrospective evaluation is appropriately done after a program has finished and the participants can reflect on the many aspects of the event. Such evaluations may be used to help guide the faculty developer in planning follow-up and new initiatives.

Keeping the Model Flexible

The Adult Learning Model for Faculty Development is meant to be a guide and assistant in the pursuit of effective faculty development. Incumbent with the stages and tasks are the principles of articulation among the stages and flexibility. This is not a model that a faculty developer gets "strapped into" with a rigid step-by-step approach. Instead, developers should find that, with the experience of actually using the model, they are modifying the tasks to fit their needs. At times, the Planning Stage may "reach back" to the Preplanning Stage task of evaluating resources as the program takes shape. Maintaining the perspective that this model is flexible and not strictly linear will enable faculty developers to reap the greatest benefits from it. The key concept here is to use the Adult Learning Model for Faculty Development as a guide and not as a restrictive harness.

Using the Faculty Development Checklist

To assist in deciding what parts of the Adult Learning Model for Faculty Development apply to specific situations and organizations, we have created the Faculty Development Checklist. (See Appendix A.) This checklist was designed to make sure that the faculty developer has a comprehensive list of things that need to be done to have successful programs. The Faculty Development Checklist is organized in a series of directives corresponding to each stage of the model. To be sure, not all of these items will apply to every situation, and additional concerns may need to be considered. However, the checklist should assist greatly in facilitating program planning in an organized and systematic way.

We recommend making copies of the checklist and distributing them to those involved in the faculty development process, such as the faculty development advisory committee or the program committee. These may be used in every stage of faculty development and will help those involved not to miss anything. We also recommend creating a file for each faculty development program. Such a file can serve as a planning journal to record specific arrangements, goals, objectives, and other pertinent information cited in the checklist. This file will be a valuable historical record not only for the present program but also for evaluation and future planning.

PROFESSIONAL DEVELOPMENT FOR THE FACULTY DEVELOPER

In establishing and delivering programs for faculty, it is important not to neglect our own roles as faculty developers. So as we bring our book to a close, we should remember that we are also adult learners. Several issues affect faculty developers personally. Attention to them will enhance our effectiveness. These issues include:

- The profession of faculty development
- Leadership
- Personal and professional development

The Profession of Faculty Development

Faculty have always striven for increased knowledge in their disciplines, and as we saw in Chapter 1, their professional life requires this continual learning. However, colleges and universities are now faced with greater challenges and this means new and demanding responsibilities for the faculty. Since the 1980s, we have seen the growth of a new profession that concerns itself solely with faculty development. Most of the interest has been centered on teaching effectiveness and learning outcomes. Colleges and universities across the country and throughout the world are creating centers whose sole purpose is to address faculty development issues and provide programming for faculty. As these centers proliferate and more and more professional educators choose the role of faculty developer we need to be aware that there has been little or no training in this area. Not many of us grow up wanting to be a faculty developer. We may come to this new professional role from a discipline such as English or science or from outside the academy. For the new faculty developer there are increasing resources and support. Networks and professional associations, such as the Professional and Organizational Development Network in Higher Education, offer literature, conferences, and on-line resources that can benefit the newcomer as well as the experienced professional. Seeking out these support systems can provide the faculty developer with new and up-to-date information on teaching and learning issues as well as delivery strategies. More importantly, they can be a source of interaction with colleagues who share similar challenges. Since faculty developers may be isolated in their institutions, professional networks and associations provide a camaraderie with mentoring opportunities we may lack within our own institutions.

Leadership

Being an effective faculty developer provides many opportunities for leadership within a college or university. We see the role of preparing and delivering faculty development initiatives as crucial to the continued enhancement of teaching and learning, and in meeting the challenges of the 21st century. This leadership role may be a new perspective for some; however, it is still important to see how leadership and program development are linked.

Throughout this book we have encouraged the faculty developer to scan the academic environment for critical issues and authentic faculty needs. This provides the opportunity to see the institution from differing perspectives and to understand holistically the workings of the academic community. With this knowledge the faculty developer is in a position to create opportunities for growth and development not only among the faculty, but also with the administration and staff as they become part of the initiative.

Leadership requires a vision, a sense of integrity, and continual learning (Bennis & Goldsmith, 1997). We have encouraged the faculty developer to be goal oriented, to understand the institution's mission, and to begin with the end in mind. Program planning can go beyond discrete presentations and sessions to encompass an overall learning agenda. The adult learning principles introduced here provide a framework in which we respect our participants, the faculty, and their unique roles. This respect means developing an awareness of who the faculty are, what their needs are, and what the needs and goals of the institution are. Each step in the process provides us with opportunities to generate support for our vision of faculty development and its intended outcome. Leaders are learners, knowing that each challenge provides opportunity for growth, new learning, and perhaps change in personal perceptions.

Professional and Personal Development

Once two lumberjacks held a wood-cutting contest. Using a large saw, one lumberjack continually sawed the wood, never stopping during the contest time. He was in a hurry to saw as much wood as he possibly could in the time allotted. The second lumberjack stopped periodically to sharpen his saw and catch his breath. Both lumberjacks had impressive piles of sawed wood. The folks observing the contest were concerned when they saw the second lumberjack stop so many times, sure that he would lose. But as the story goes, this lumberjack in the end sawed more wood and won the contest. His sharp saw made the difference as it was more efficient in getting the job done.

The moral of the story, drawn from Stephen Covey (1989), is that we need to take time out from our tasks to sharpen our saw, that is, to get renewed, refreshed, and reenergized. We agree with Covey's advice and urge faculty developers to build in time for sharpening their saws. We would add reflection and learning to Covey's list of things to do during that time out.

Schön's (1983) concept of the reflective practitioner was introduced in Chapter 3; this theme has permeated our model. Taking time out for reflection, knowing what we are doing, and understanding why we are doing it are all central to our own professional and personal development. Brookfield (1986) reminds us that as program planners we need to be "consistently innovative and adaptive" (p. 248), which requires us to understand who we are as professional faculty developers and how we are effective in that role. In Chapter 6, one of the tasks to complete is an assessment of the faculty developer's role. Taking the time out for this assessment during and after the planning is essential, which is why we have included it in the model and have provided an assessment tool in Appendix B.

Covey's story reminds us that we too should be learning. Of course, with each new program we plan, we do learn something new, but we suggest more formal learning initiatives. The growing literature on faculty development offers effective teaching strategies and examples of successful faculty development programs. Our references offer an extensive list of books and articles on these topics. Professional networks and associations also have periodicals, newsletters, journals, and monographs with practical information and up-to-date practice examples. Professional associations sponsor conferences, institutes, and training. The *Chronicle of Higher Education*, a weekly publication covering news and issues in higher education, provides notices and advertisements of such upcoming events. Within our own institutions we may find a wealth of resources among our own faculty. The Department of Education would be a good place to start. Faculty working in the areas of motivation, adult learning, curriculum development, and instructional technology can be enlisted to help initiate and deliver programming, and may also be a source of mentoring and professional development.

Whether new to faculty development or seasoned practitioners, we may find a personal development plan helpful. It directs our thinking by posing the following questions. What are my goals for this position and this work? What do I want to accomplish both personally and professionally? How will I assess my effectiveness as a faculty developer? What strategies will provide opportunities to continued success? What challenges do I see for myself? How will I grow and develop? Looking at long-term goals and what we want to accomplish is helpful in evaluating a personal mission and philosophy. As professionals we will bring our education, our experiences, our intellect and creativity, and our temperaments to the work of faculty development. Are we clear about our own values when it comes to educating adults? Answering these questions, along with using the Faculty Developer's Self-Assessment Tool in Appendix B, can provide a sense of direction and a plan for personal development.

In closing, we have some advice for all faculty developers. We have both been in the faculty development trenches as developers and as participants in many programs. We have learned a lot from our own experiences, and being true to adult learning principles, we believe that this experience should be taken into consideration. First of all, we say, be flexible. Working with human beings demands it. Whether the fire alarm goes off during presentation or the computer won't accept the multimedia show, we need to understand things will not always go the way we planned. Building in contingencies, being creative at the last minute, and never underestimating the complexities of human interaction are essential for effective faculty development. On a more positive note, participants bring a wealth of experience and information to an educational event. We must be ready to take advantage of it. We can enjoy the contributions of the participants and help those working with us to understand this is a valuable resource and one that should be encouraged.

Second, we must learn to live with disappointments. Even

the best-planned program may have unintended outcomes for some participants. We cannot always foresee natural events and emergencies which may disrupt our programs. These events will happen. Blizzards cancel workshops, presenters fail to follow our guidance, and participants are not always as enthusiastic as we had hoped. We all occasionally encounter such interference when presenting programming.

Faculty development is a risk-taking endeavor and along with risks may come disappointments, which brings us to our third piece of advice, we need to have a sense of humor. Program planning is creative, exciting, and fun. It provides us with the opportunity to initiate change and to make a difference. To meet these challenges we can see them either as hurdles or as prospects for enhancing the work of our institution and our profession. Having a sense of humor, not taking ourselves too seriously, and seeing the positive aspects of our work provide us with not only stress reduction, but also a model for those around us to observe and perhaps emulate. If we can laugh after the fire drill is over, we will reduce tension and model effective leadership. Remember that faculty, by their very nature of their profession, are lifelong learners in their disciplines. Now it is our opportunity to help them in a positive way expand their lifelong learning to other areas by using the Adult Learning Model for Faculty Development which respects them as adult learners and incorporates principles to facilitate the learning process.

Ultimately, it is our desire that faculty development in higher education benefit from looking at the faculty development process from an adult learning perspective. While endeavoring to improve teaching and learning on college campuses, the needs and promise of the faculty as adult learners provide a foundation for successful faculty development initiatives.

APPENDIX A

Faculty Development Checklist

Preplanning

_____ **Understanding Organizational Culture**
_____ List reasons for doing faculty development in general.
_____ List reasons for this specific faculty development program.
_____ Identify the initiator(s) of the faculty development.
_____ Scan the institutional climate.
_____ Review the history of faculty development within the institution.
_____ Ascertain how faculty development is perceived on campus by faculty and administration.
_____ Determine the success/failure of previous faculty development programs.
_____ Identify all who should be involved.
_____ Decide if an advisory committee would be appropriate.
_____ Identify and invite advisory committee members.
_____ Review the mission and goals of the organization and how it relates to faculty development.

_____ **Identifying the Role of the Faculty Developer**
_____ Review your philosophy of education.
_____ List your experience and training that can be applied to faculty development.
_____ Explore your values regarding professional development.
_____ Assess your connections and relationships across the institution that may impact this process.

_____ **Assessing Needs**
_____ Identify the faculty's perceived and real needs.
_____ Identify the institution's perceived and real needs.
_____ Select the appropriate needs assessment process.
_____ Collect needs assessment.
_____ Analyze data and prioritize needs.
_____ Ascertain how identified needs coincide or conflict with institutional culture.

_____ **Evaluating Resources**
_____ List the human, physical, and financial resources needed for faculty development.
_____ Identify the available resources.
_____ Identify the sources of additional resources that may be needed.
_____ Ascertain if support, real and intangible, is available.
_____ Construct a budget.

_____ **Establishing Goals**
_____ Select program objectives based on the needs assessment.
_____ Review anticipated outcomes.
_____ Write program goals.
_____ Create benchmarks for measuring goal achievement.
_____ Write a directional plan based on the following questions:
    _____ What do you want the faculty to be able to do when the event is over?
    _____ What changes do you hope to accomplish with the faculty and within the organization?
    _____ How will you know you have achieved your goals?

Planning

_____ **Selecting a Topic**
_____ Review needs assessment data.
_____ Assess resources, people, and organizational concerns.
_____ Select appropriate content.

_____ **Identifying a Presenter**
_____ Review budget.
_____ Involve advisory committee.
_____ Review potential presenters both on and off campus.
_____ Assess the appropriateness of the presenter to the topic.
_____ Consider presentation skills and delivery methods of the presenter.
_____ Ascertain if the presenter will tailor the program to fit faculty and institutional needs.

_____ **Preparing for Delivery**
_____ Work with the presenter to incorporate faculty needs and adult learning principles.
_____ Plan for the incorporation of adult learning principles.
_____ Plan for learner involvement in the program.
_____ Determine appropriate teaching techniques.

_____ **Preparing for Support and Transfer of Learning**
_____ Assess the environmental climate for support.
_____ Review resources for support.
_____ Identify obstacles to transfer of learning.
_____ Align faculty development efforts with the mission of the institution.

_____ **Scheduling the Event**
_____ Review academic calendar.
_____ Consider faculty schedules.
_____ Confer with advisory committee.
_____ Include faculty in selecting date and time for the faculty development program.

_____ **Beginning the Evaluation**
_____ Review the purpose of evaluation.
_____ Choose areas to be evaluated both during and at the end of the program.
_____ Incorporate a design review.
_____ Develop a formative evaluation plan.

_____ Determine evaluation methods to be considered for this program.

_____ Plan for collecting data at the end of the program.

Delivery

_____ Building on the Preparation

_____ Review goals and objectives.

_____ Step back and assess overall picture of the program.

_____ Reassess faculty and institutional needs.

_____ Promoting the Program

_____ Develop a plan for marketing the program.

_____ Prepare a timeline for promoting the program.

_____ Create publicity materials.

_____ Identify effective channels for distributing publicity materials.

_____ Provide opportunities for registration.

_____ Elicit support from institutional sources.

_____ Implementing Adult Learning Principles

_____ Revisit adult learning principles:

   _____ Create a climate of respect.

   _____ Encourage active participation.

   _____ Build on experience.

   _____ Employ collaborate inquiry.

   _____ Learn for action.

   _____ Empower participants.

_____ Incorporate learner-centered concepts into the program.

_____ Ensure that faculty needs are being considered.

_____ Utilize the experiences of the faculty to enhance learning.

_____ Assess whether the content and delivery of the program are relevant to faculty needs.

_____ Monitoring the Program

_____ Engage in evaluative functions throughout the program.

_____ Be present and available for troubleshooting, with attention to the following:
 _____ Schedule and timing
 _____ Room arrangements
 _____ Traffic flow
 _____ Room temperature and ventilation
 _____ Equipment needs:
  _____ Set-up
  _____ Troubleshooting
 _____ Refreshments
_____ Have contingency plans available for anticipated problems.
_____ Gather data to summarize the program experience.

Follow-up

_____ **Evaluating**
_____ Design an appropriate summative evaluation plan.
_____ Identify questions evaluation data should answer.
_____ Select appropriate evaluation methods.
_____ Collect evaluation data.
_____ Elicit feedback from the advisory committee.
_____ Analyze evaluation data.
_____ Incorporate formative evaluation data.
_____ Prepare and distribute reports to all stakeholders.

_____ **Continuing the Learning**
_____ Assess for transfer of learning.
_____ Engage in a continual needs assessment process among the faculty.
_____ Observe the support for implementation of new skills and learning.
_____ Align goals of learning with reward systems.
_____ Ensure faculty are supported through change.
_____ Initiate collaborative opportunities for support.
_____ Create opportunities for networking.

_____ **Assessing the Faculty Developer's Role**

_____ Summarize the process from a holistic and retrospective position.

_____ Reflect on learning outcomes and changes.

_____ Incorporate the evaluation reports.

_____ Complete the self-assessment tool.

_____ Invite perceptions and assessment from constituents throughout the institution.

_____ Elicit observations from advisory committee.

_____ Integrate assessment and reflection information.

APPENDIX B

Faculty Developer's Self-Assessment Tool

Faculty developers should take time to reflect on their work and programs. These questions may be answered as the faculty development initiative draws to a close. Take some time and reflect on the experience and write down your responses. If you have been keeping a learning autobiography, review your entries and include your thoughts in this self-assessment.

The Faculty Development Program

1. Thinking back over the entire faculty development program, in what ways was it successful?

   What contributed to this success?

2. Now, think back again, in what ways was it unsuccessful?

   What contributed to the difficulties encountered?

3. Describe your satisfaction with the outcome of the faculty development initiative.

4. To what extent have the stated goals and objectives been met through this faculty development initiative?

5. List five things that you would definitely do again when planning and delivering a faculty development program.

6. List five things that you would definitely NOT do again.

7. What was your biggest challenge in this instance? Describe why it was such a challenge.

8. The next time you plan for faculty development, how would you meet this challenge?

Your Role as a Faculty Developer:

1. How did you succeed in your role as an effective faculty developer?

2. What limitations did you have this time as an effective faculty developer?

3. What one thing can you do for yourself as a faculty developer to increase the effectiveness of your next program?

4. What can you do to increase your enjoyment of your role as a faculty developer?

REFERENCES

Angelo, T. A. (1994, June). From faculty development to academic development. *American Association of Higher Education (AAHE) Bulletin*, 3-7.

Apps, J. W. (1991). *Mastering the teaching of adults*. Malabar, FL: Krieger.

Baiocco, S. A., & DeWaters, J. N. (1995, September-October). Futuristic faculty development: A collegiate development network. *Academe*, 38-39.

Baiocco, S. A., & DeWaters, J. N. (1998). *Successful college teaching: Problem-solving strategies of distinguished professors*. Boston: Allyn & Bacon.

Baldwin, T. T., & Ford, J. K. (1988). Transfer of training: A review and directions for future research. *Personnel Psychology, 41*, 63-105.

Bee, H. L. (1996). *The journey of adulthood* (3rd ed.). Englewood Cliffs, NJ: Prentice Hall.

Bennis, W., & Goldsmith, J. (1997). *Learning to lead: A workbook on becoming a leader*. Reading, MA: Addison-Wesley.

Bergquist, W. H. (1992). *The four cultures of the academy: Insights and strategies for improving leadership in collegiate organizations*. San Francisco: Jossey-Bass.

Birnbaum, R. (1988). *How colleges work: The cybernetics of academic organization and leadership*. San Francisco: Jossey-Bass.

Blackburn, R. T., & Lawrence, J. H. (1995). *Faculty at work: Motivation, expectation, satisfaction*. Baltimore: The John Hopkins University Press.

Boice, R. (1992). *The new faculty member: Supporting and fostering professional development*. San Francisco: Jossey-Bass.

Boyle, P. G. (1981). *Planning better programs*. New York: McGraw-Hill.

Brew, A. (1995). Trends and influences. In A. Brew (Ed.), *Directions in staff development* (pp. 1–16). Bristol, PA: The Society for Research into Higher Education.

Broad, M. L. (1997). Transfer concepts and research overview: Challenges for organizational performance. In M. L. Broad (Ed.), *Transferring learning to the workplace* (pp. 1–18). Alexandria, VA: American Society for Training and Development.

Brockett, R. G. (Ed.). (1988). *Ethical issues in adult education.* New York: Teachers College Press.

Brockett, R. G. (1991). Professional development, artistry and style. In R. G. Brockett (Ed.), *Professional development of educators of adults* (pp. 5–14). New Directions in Adult and Continuing Education (No. 51). San Francisco: Jossey-Bass.

Brookfield, S. D. (1986). *Understanding and facilitating adult learning.* San Francisco: Jossey-Bass.

Brookfield, S. D. (1990). *The skillful teacher.* San Francisco: Jossey-Bass.

Brookfield, S. D. (1995). *Becoming a critically reflective teacher.* San Francisco: Jossey-Bass.

Brown, S. M., & Seidner, C. J. (Eds.). (1998). *Evaluating corporate training: Models and issues.* Boston: Kluwer Academic Publishers.

Caffarella, R. S. (1988). *Program development and evaluation resource book for trainers.* New York: Wiley.

Caffarella, R. S. (1994). *Planning programs for adult learners: A practical guide for educators, trainers, and staff developers.* San Francisco: Jossey-Bass.

Candy, P. C. (1996). Promoting lifelong learning: Academic developers and the university as a learning organization. *International Journal for Academic Development, 1* (1), 7–18.

Carroll, R. G. (1993). Implications of adult education theories for medical school faculty development programs. *Medical Teacher, 15* (2/3), 163–170.

Cervero, R. M., & Wilson, A. L. (1994). *Planning responsibly for adult education: A guide to negotiating power and interests.* San Francisco: Jossey-Bass.

Cervero, R. M., & Wilson, A. L. (Eds.). (1996). *What really happens in adult education program planning: Lessons in negotiating power and interests.* New Directions for Adult and Continuing Education (No. 69). San Francisco: Jossey-Bass.

Chen, H. (1990). *Theory-driven evaluations.* San Francisco: Sage.

Chism, N. V. N., & Szabo, B. (1997–1998). How faculty development programs evaluate their services. *The Journal of Staff, Program, & Organization Development, 15* (2), 55–62.

Ciulla, J. B. (1998). Leadership and the problem of bogus empowerment. In J. B. Ciulla (Ed.), *Ethics: The heart of leadership* (pp. 63–86). Westport, CT: Praeger.

Cookson, P. S. (1998). *Program planning for the training and continuing education of adults: North American perspectives.* Malabar, FL: Krieger.

Covey, S. R. (1989). *The seven habits of highly effective people: Restoring the character ethic.* New York: Fireside Simon & Schuster.

Cox, M. (1994–1995). Emerging trends in college teaching for the 21st century. *Teaching Excellence Toward the Best in the Academy, 6* (6).

Cranton, P. (1994). *Understanding and promoting transformative learning: A guide for educators of adults.* San Francisco: Jossey-Bass.

Cranton, P. (1996). *Professional development as perspective transformation.* San Francisco: Jossey-Bass.

Cranton, P. (Ed.). (1997). *Transformative learning in action: Insights from practice.* New Directions in Adult and Continuing Education (No. 74). San Francisco: Jossey-Bass.

Crawley, A. L. (1995). Faculty development programs at research universities: Implications for senior faculty renewal. *To Improve the Academy, 14,* 65–90.

Cross, K. P. (1981). *Adults as learners: Increasing participation and facilitating learning.* San Francisco: Jossey-Bass.

Eble, K. E., & McKeachie, W. J. (1985). *Improving undergraduate education through faculty development: An analysis of effective programs and practices.* San Francisco: Jossey-Bass.

Ekroth, L. (1990, Winter-Spring). Why professors don't change. *Teaching Excellence: Toward the Best in the Academy.*

Elias, J. L., & Merriam, S. B. (1995). *Philosophical foundations of adult education* (2nd ed.). Malabar, FL: Krieger.

Gadotti, M. (1994). *Reading Paulo Freire: His life and work.* Albany, NY: State University of New York Press.

Gaff, J. G. (1976). *Toward faculty renewal.* San Francisco: Jossey-Bass.

Gaff, J. G., & Simpson, R. D. (1994). Faculty development in the United States. *Innovative Higher Education, 18* (3), 167–176.

Galbraith, M. W. (Ed.). (1998). *Adult learning methods* (2nd ed.). Malabar, FL: Krieger.

Galbraith, M. W., Sisco, B. R., & Guglielmino, L. M. (1997). *Administering successful programs for adults: Promoting excellence in adult, community, and continuing education.* Malabar, FL: Krieger.

Gordon, G. H., & Levinson, W. (1990). Attitudes toward learner-centered learning at a faculty development course. *Teaching and Learning in Medicine, 2* (2), 106–109.

Halpern, D. F., & Associates. (1994). *Changing college classrooms: New teaching and learning strategies for an increasingly complex world.* San Francisco: Jossey-Bass.

Hawthorne, E. M., & Smith, A. B. (1994). Continuing development of community college faculty. In A. M. Hoffaman & D. J. Julius (Eds.), *Managing community and junior colleges: Perspectives for the next century* (pp. 180–187). Washington, DC: The College and University Personnel Association.

Hiemstra, R. (1988). Translating personal values and philosophy into practical action. In R. G. Brockett (Ed.), *Ethical issues in adult education* (pp. 178–194). New York: Teachers College Press.

Hubbard, G. T., & Atkins, S. S. (1995). The professor as a person: The role of faculty well-being in faculty development. *Innovative Higher Education, 20* (2), 117–127.

Imel, S. (1991). Ethical practice in adult education. *ERIC Digest No. 116.* Columbus, OH: ERIC Clearinghouse on Adult, Career, and Vocational Education, The Ohio State University.

Jarvis, P. (1995). *Adult and continuing education: Theory and practice.* New York: Routledge.

Katz, J., & Henry, M. (1996). *Turning professors into teachers: A new approach to faculty development and student learning.* Phoenix, AZ: Oryx Press.

King, K. P. (1997). Examining learning activities and transformational learning. *International Journal of University Adult Education, 36* (3), 23–37.

King, K. P. (1998a). Course development on the World Wide Web. In B. Cahoon (Ed.), *Adult learning and the Internet* (pp. 25–31). New Directions for Adult and Continuing Education (No. 78). San Francisco: Jossey-Bass.

King, K. P. (1998b). Keeping pace with technology: Guidelines for empowering teachers with technology skills. *Impact on Instructional Improvement, 27* (2), 13–20.

King, K. P. (1998c). *A guide to perspective transformation and learning activities: The learning activities survey.* Philadelphia: Research for Better Schools.

King, K. P. (1999, Fall). Unleashing technology in the classroom: What adult basic education teachers and organizations need to know. *Adult Basic Education: An Interdisciplinary Journal for Adult Literacy Educators, 9* (3), 162–175.

King, K. P., & Lawler, P. A. (1998). Institutional and individual support of growth among adult learners. *New Horizons in Adult Education, 12* (1), 4–11.

Kirkpatrick, D. L. (1998). The four levels of evaluation. In S. M. Brown & C. J. Seidner (Eds.), *Evaluating corporate training: Models and issues* (pp. 95–112). Boston: Kluwer Academic Publishers.

Knapper, C. K. (1995). Understanding student learning: Implications for instructional practice. In W. A. Wright & Associates. *Teaching improvement practices: Successful strategies for higher education* (pp. 58–75). Boston: Anker.

Knowles, M. S. (1980). *The modern practice of adult education: From andragogy to pedagogy* (2nd ed.). New York: Cambridge.

Knowles, M. S. (1989). *The making of an adult educator: An autobiographical journey.* San Francisco: Jossey-Bass.

Knowles, M. S. (1992). *The adult learner: A neglected species* (4th ed.). Houston: Gulf.

Knox, A. (1986). *Helping adults learn: A guide to planning, implementing and conducting programs.* San Francisco: Jossey-Bass.

Kotler, P., & Andreasen, A. R. (1987). *Strategic marketing for nonprofit organizations* (3rd ed.). Englewood Cliffs, NJ: Prentice Hall.

Kowalski, T. J. (1988). *The organization and planning of adult education.* Albany, NY: State University of New York.

Kozlowski, S. W. J. (1995). Organizational change, informal learning, and adaptation: Emerging trends in training and continuing education. *The Journal of Continuing Higher Education, 43* (1), 2–11.

Lawler, P. A. (1991). *The keys of adult learning: Theory and practical strategies.* Philadelphia: Research for Better Schools.

Lawler, P. A. (1998). The ethics of evaluating training. In S. M. Brown & C. J. Seidner (Eds.), *Evaluating corporate training: Models and issues* (pp. 237–256). Boston: Kluwer Academic Publishers.

Lawler, P. A., DeCosmo, A. D., & Wilhite, S. C. (1996). Faculty awareness and use of adult learning principles. In H. Reno & M. Witte (Eds.), *37th Annual Adult Education Research Conference Proceedings* (pp. 212–216). Tampa, FL: University of South Florida.

Lawler, P., & Fielder, J. (1991). Analyzing ethical problems in continuing higher education: A model for practical use. *The Journal of Continuing Higher Education, 39* (2), 20–25.

Lawler, P. A., & Wilhite, S. C. (1997). Catching up with the information age: A new paradigm for faculty development. *22nd International Conference Improving University Learning and Teaching Conference Proceedings* (pp. 369–378). Rio de Janeiro, Brazil: Faculdade da Cidade & University of Maryland University College.

Lewis, R. G., & Smith, D. H. (1994). *Total quality in higher education.* Delray Beach, FL: St. Lucia Press.

Licklider, B. E., Schnelker, D. L., & Fulton, C. (1997–1998). Revisioning faculty development for changing times: The foundation and framework. *The Journal of Staff, Program & Organizational Development, 15* (3), 121–133.

Lindeman, E. C. (1961). *The meaning of adult education.* Norman, OK: Oklahoma Research Center for Continuing Professional and Higher Education.

Luce, J. A., & Murray, J. P. (1997–1998). New faculty's perceptions of the academic work life. *The Journal of Staff, Program, & Organization Development, 15* (3), 103–110.

Maxwell, W. E., & Kazlauskas, E. J. (1992). Which faculty development methods really work in community colleges? A review of research. *Community/Junior College Quarterly, 16,* 351–360.

Merriam, S. B., & Brockett, R. G. (1997). *The profession and practice of adult education: An introduction.* San Francisco: Jossey-Bass.

Merriam, S. B., & Caffarella, R. S. (1992). *Learning in adulthood.* San Francisco: Jossey-Bass.

Merriam, S. B., & Caffarella, R. S. (1999). *Learning in adulthood* (2nd ed.). San Francisco: Jossey-Bass.

Meyers, C., & Jones, T. B. (1993). *Promoting active learning: Strategies for the college classroom.* San Francisco: Jossey-Bass.

Mezirow, J., & Associates. (1990). *Fostering critical reflection in adulthood: A guide to transformative and emancipatory learning.* San Francisco: Jossey-Bass.

Millis, B. J. (1994). Faculty development in the 1990s: What it is and why we can't wait. *Journal of Counseling & Development, 72,* 454–464.

Mills, D. P., Cervero, R. M., Langone, C. A., & Wilson, A. L. (1995). The impact of interests, power relationships, and organizational structure on program planning practice: A case study. *Adult Education Quarterly, 46* (1), 1–16.

Morgan, M. M., Phelps, P. H., & Pritchard, J. E. (1995). Credibility: The crux of faculty development. *To Improve the Academy, 14,* 57–63.

Murk, P. J., & Galbraith, M. W. (1986). Planning successful continuing education programs: A systems approach model. *Lifelong Learning Journal, 9* (5), 21–23.

Murk, P. J., & Walls, J. L. (1997). *The planning wheel: Value added performance.* Paper presented at the 46th Annual American Association for Adult and Continuing Education Conference, Cincinnati, OH.

Paulsen, M. B., & Feldman, K. A. (1995). *Taking teaching seriously: Meeting the challenge of instructional improvement.* ASHE-ERIC Higher Education Report No. 2, Washington, DC: The George Washington University, Graduate School of Education and Human Development.

Parrott, W. (1998). Formative evaluation. In S. M. Brown & C. J. Seidner (Eds.), *Evaluating corporate training: Models and issues* (pp. 167–182). Boston: Kluwer Academic Publishers.

Peters, J. M. (1991). Strategies for reflective practice. In R. G. Brockett (Ed.), *Professional development for educators of adults* (pp. 89–94). New Directions for Adult and Continuing Education (No. 51). San Francisco: Jossey-Bass.

Posavac, E. J., & Carey, R. G. (1992). *Program evaluation: Methods and case studies* (4th ed.). Englewood Cliffs, NJ: Prentice Hall.

Rowley, D. J., Lujan, H. D., & Dolence, M. G. (1997). *Strategic change in colleges and universities: Planning to survive and prosper.* San Francisco: Jossey-Bass.

Schneider, B., & Zalesny, M. D. (1982). Human needs and faculty motivation. In J. L. Bess (Ed.), *Motivating professors to teach effectively* (pp. 37–46). New Directions for Teaching and Learning (No. 10). San Francisco: Jossey-Bass.

Schön, D. A. (1983). *The reflective practitioner: How professionals think in action.* New York: Basic Books.

Seldin, P. (1990). Summary and recommendations. In P. Seldin & Associates. *How administrators can improve teaching: Moving from talk to action in higher education* (pp. 199–213). San Francisco: Jossey-Bass.

Silberman, M. (1996). *Active learning: 101 strategies to teach any subject.* Needham Heights, MA: Allyn & Bacon.

Simerly, R., & Associates. (1989). *Handbook of marketing for continuing education.* San Francisco: Jossey-Bass.

Simpson, E. L. (1990). *Faculty renewal in higher education.* Malabar, FL: Krieger.

Smylie, M. A. (1995). Teacher learning in the workplace: Implications for school reform. In T. R. Guskey & M. Huberman (Eds.), *Professional development in education: New paradigms and practices* (pp. 92–113). New York: Teachers College Press.

Sorcinelli, M. D. (1994). Effective approaches to new faculty development. *Journal of Counseling & Development, 72,* 474–479.

Sork, T. J. (1988). Ethical issues in program planning. In R. G. Brockett (Ed.), *Ethical issues in adult education* (pp. 34–49). New York: Teachers College Press.

Sork, T. J. (1991). *Mistakes made and lessons learned: Overcoming obstacles to successful program planning.* New Directions for Adult and Continuing Education (No. 49). San Francisco: Jossey-Bass.

Sork, T. J., & Buskey, J. H. (1986). A description and evaluation analysis of program planning literature, 1950–1983. *Adult Education Quarterly, 36* (2), 86–96.

Taylor, K., & Marineau, C. (Eds.). (1995). *Learning environments for women's adult development: Bridges toward change.* New Directions for Adult and Continuing Education (No. 65). San Francisco: Jossey-Bass.

Tyler, R. W. (1949). *Basic principles of curriculum and instruction.* Chicago: University of Chicago Press.

Teitel, L. (1994). *The advisory committee advantage: Creating an effective strategy for programmatic improvement.* ASHE-ERIC Higher Education Report No. 1. Washington, DC: The George Washington University School of Education and Human Development.

Uhland, R. (1994). Social policy and adult education program planning: Perspectives on Tyler and Boyle models. *PAACE Journal of Lifelong Learning,* (3), 62–70.

Walker, K. (1993, November/December). Values, ethics and ethical decision making. *Adult Learning,* 13–14.

Watkins, K. E., & Marsick, V. J. (1993). *Sculpting the learning organization: Lessons in the art and science of systemic change.* San Francisco: Jossey-Bass.

Watson, G., & Grossman, L. H. (1994). Pursuing a comprehensive faculty development program: Making fragmentation work. *Journal of Counseling and Development, 72,* 465–473.

Wedman, J., & Strathe, M. (1985, February). Faculty development in technology: A model for higher education. *Educational Technology,* 15–19.

Weimer, M. (1990). *Improving college teaching: Strategies for developing instructional effectiveness.* San Francisco: Jossey-Bass.

Wilhite, S. C., DeCosmo, A. D., & Lawler, P. A. (1996). Faculty as adult learners: Implications for faculty development initiatives. *The Eastern Adult, Continuing and Distance Education Research Conference Proceedings.* The Pennsylvania State University, University Park, PA, October, (CD-ROM).

Wilms, W. W., & Moore, R. W. (Eds.). (1987). *Marketing strategies of changing times.* New Directions for Community Colleges (No. 60). San Francisco: Jossey-Bass.

Wilson, A. L., & Cervero, R. M. (1997, March-April). The song remains the same: The selective tradition of technical rationality in adult education program planning theory. *International Journal of Lifelong Education, 16* (2), 84–108.

Wlodkowski, R. J. (1993). *Enhancing adult motivation to learn: A guide to improving instruction and increasing learner achievement.* San Francisco: Jossey-Bass.

Zinn, L. M. (1993, November/December). Do the right thing. Ethical decision making in professional and business practice. *Adult Learning,* 7–8.

Zinn, L. M., (1998). Identifying your philosophical orientation. In M. W. Galbraith (Ed.), *Adult learning methods* (2nd ed.). (pp. 37–72). Malabar, FL: Krieger.

INDEX